# ALL ABOUT EVE

# ALL ABOUT EVE

A screenplay by

JOSEPH L. MANKIEWICZ

Based upon a short story by MARY ORR

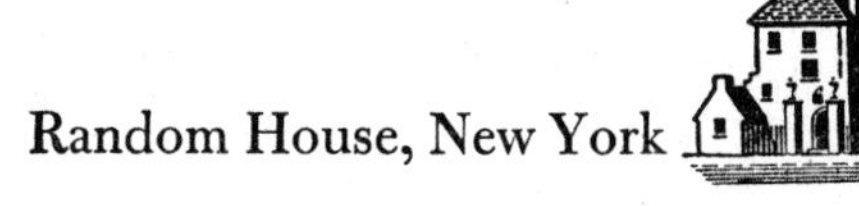

Random House, New York

First Printing





*All About Eve* is a work of the imagination and all
the characters and events therein are fictional.
Any resemblance to persons, living or dead, is entirely coincidental.



MANUFACTURED IN THE UNITED STATES OF AMERICA

For Rosa —

The Critic on My Hearth

| | |
|---|---|
| PRODUCED BY | Darryl F. Zanuck |
| WRITTEN FOR THE SCREEN AND DIRECTED BY | Joseph L. Mankiewicz |
| MUSIC | Alfred Newman |
| DIRECTOR OF PHOTOGRAPHY | Milton Krasner, ASC |
| ART DIRECTION | Lyle Wheeler, George W. Davis |
| SET DECORATIONS | Thomas Little, Walter M. Scott |
| FILM EDITOR | Barbara McLean |
| WARDROBE DIRECTION | Charles Le Maire |
| COSTUMES FOR MISS BETTE DAVIS | Designed by Edith Head |
| ORCHESTRATION | Edward Powell |
| MAKEUP ARTIST | Ben Nye |
| SPECIAL PHOTOGRAPHIC EFFECTS | Fred Sersen |
| SOUND | W. D. Flick, Roger Heman |

## CAST

| | |
|---|---|
| MARGO CHANNING | Bette Davis |
| EVE HARRINGTON | Anne Baxter |
| ADDISON DE WITT | George Sanders |
| KAREN RICHARDS | Celeste Holm |
| BILL SAMPSON | Gary Merrill |
| LLOYD RICHARDS | Hugh Marlowe |
| BIRDIE | Thelma Ritter |
| MISS CASWELL | Marilyn Monroe |
| MAX FABIAN | Gregory Ratoff |
| PHOEBE | Barbara Bates |
| AGED ACTOR | Walter Hampden |

*All About Eve* was first presented by Twentieth Century-Fox Film Corporation at the Roxy Theatre, New York City, on October 13, 1950.

# FOREWORD

One of the most common misconceptions about a filmscript is an apprehension that it is a highly technical blueprint made up of incomprehensible symbols, graphs and charts — and that the dialogue is rather casually made up by the actors as they go along. It is true that some actors, under a delusion of literacy, try to tamper with written words. It is also true that occasionally writers indulge in flights of technical fancy which might include anything from designating a particular camera lens to instructions for parting the Red Sea in miniature.

There is some reason for the latter. Inasmuch as his filmscript may be on the stage many months after he has written it, and inasmuch as he may be not only mentally but geographically remote from it, the writer's voluminous technical exhortations act sometimes within his filmscript as a sort of last testament — as a plea, by remote control, for a voice in what goes on the screen, and how it gets there.

The privilege of directing my own scripts has enabled me to use even less technical terminology than is usual. Another and more important reason is the simple fact that I have never been able to learn or understand a great deal about it. The craftsmen in the production and technical departments of the studios are incomparably gifted. By throwing himself, in humble trust, upon their experience and craftsmanship, the director can emerge repeatedly with feats of technical accomplishment for which he will receive much kudos and which he could not possibly have attained on his own.

However, in order to make clear even those few technical terms I do use, herewith a short glossary:

FADE IN and FADE OUT. The equivalent of raising and lowering the curtain to signify the start and finish of an act in a play.

The DISSOLVE can best be described, for reading purposes, as a means of separating scenes within an act without lowering the curtain. Comparable to, let us say, a dimming of the lights . . .

J. L. M.

# ALL ABOUT EVE

FADE IN

DINING HALL — SARAH SIDDONS SOCIETY — NIGHT

It is not a large room and jammed with tables; mostly for four but some for six and eight. A long table of honor, for about thirty people, has been placed upon a dais.

Dinner is over. Demi-tasses, cigars and brandy. The over-all effect is one of worn elegance and dogged gentility. It is June.

The CAMERA, as it has been throughout the CREDIT TITLES, is on a

FULL CLOSEUP

of the SARAH SIDDONS AWARD. It is a gold statuette, about a foot high, of Sarah Siddons as "The Tragic Muse." Exquisitely framed in a nest of flowers, it rests on a miniature altar in the center of the table of honor.

OVER THIS we hear the crisp, cultured, precise VOICE of ADDISON DEWITT:

ADDISON'S VOICE

*The Sarah Siddons Award for Distinguished*

*Achievement is perhaps unknown to you. It has been spared the sensational and commercial publicity that attends such questionable "honors" as the Nobel Prize — and those awards presented annually by that film society . . .*

The CAMERA has EASED BACK to include some of the table of honor and a distinguished gentleman with snow-white hair who is speaking. He is a few years either side of 100. We do not hear what he says.

ADDISON'S VOICE

*The distinguished-looking gentleman is an extremely old actor. Being an actor, he will go on speaking for some time. It is not important that you hear what he says.*

The CAMERA EASES BACK some more, and CONTINUES until it discloses a fairly COMPREHENSIVE SHOT of the room.

ADDISON'S VOICE

*However, it is important that you know where you are, and why you are here. This is the dining hall of the Sarah Siddons Society. The occasion is its annual banquet and presentation of the highest honor our Theatre knows — the Sarah Siddons Award for Distinguished Achievement.*

A GROUP OF WAITERS

Clustered near the screens masking the entrances to the kitchen. The screens are papered with old theatrical programs. The waiters are all aged and venerable. They look respectfully toward the speaker . . .

ADDISON'S VOICE

*These hallowed walls, indeed many of these faces, have looked upon Modjeska, Ada Rehan and Minnie Fiske. Mansfield's voice filled this room. Booth breathed this air. It is unlikely that the windows have been opened since his death.*

CLOSE — THE AWARD

On its altar, it shines proudly above five or six smaller altars which surround it and which are now empty.

ADDISON'S VOICE

*The minor awards, as you can see, have already been presented. Minor awards are for such as the writer and director—since their function is merely to construct a tower so that the world can applaud a light which flashes on top of it . . .*

(the CAMERA MOVES to an EXTREME CLOSEUP of the Award)

*. . . and no brighter light has ever dazzled the eye than Eve Harrington. Eve. But more of Eve, later. All about Eve, in fact . . .*

CLOSE — ADDISON DE WITT

Not young, not unattractive, a fastidious dresser, sharp of eye and merciless of tongue. An omnipresent cigarette holder projects from his mouth like the sword of D'Artagnan.

He sits back in his chair, musingly, his fingers making little cannonballs out of bread crumbs. His narration covers the MOVE of the CAMERA to him:

ADDISON'S VOICE

*To those of you who do not read, attend the theatre, listen to unsponsored radio programs or know anything of the world in which you live — it is perhaps necessary to introduce myself.*

(CAMERA IS ON him now)

*My name is Addison DeWitt. My native habitat is the Theatre — in it I toil not, neither do I spin. I am a critic and commentator. I am essential to the Theatre — as ants to a picnic, as the boll weevil to a cotton field . . .*

He looks to his left. The CAMERA MOVES to a

CLOSEUP — KAREN RICHARDS

She is lovely and thirtyish in an unprofessional way. She is scraping bread crumbs, spilled sugar, etc., into a little pile with a spoon. Addison takes one of her bread crumbs. She smiles absently . . .

CLOSEUP — ADDISON

He rolls the bread crumb into a cannonball.

ADDISON'S VOICE

*This is Karen Richards. She is the wife of a playwright, therefore of the Theatre by marriage. Nothing in her background or breeding should have brought her any closer to the stage than row E, center . . .*

CLOSEUP — KAREN

She continues her doodling.

ADDISON'S VOICE

*. . . however, during her senior year at Radcliffe, Lloyd Richards lectured on the drama. The following year Karen became Mrs. Lloyd Richards. Lloyd is the author of* Footsteps on the Ceiling, *the play which has won for Eve Harrington the Sarah Siddons Award . . .*

Karen absently pats the top of her little pile of refuse. A hand reaches in to take the spoon away. Karen looks as the CAMERA PANS with IT to a

CLOSEUP — MAX FABIAN

He sits at her left. He's a sad-faced man with glasses and a look of constant apprehension. He smiles apologetically and indicates a white powder which he unwraps. He pantomimes that his ulcer is snapping.

CLOSE — KAREN

She smiles back, returns to her doodling.

CLOSE — ADDISON

He mashes a cigarette stub, pops it out of his holder. He eyes Max.

ADDISON'S VOICE

*There are in general two types of theatrical producers. One has a great many wealthy friends who will risk a tax-deductible loss. This type is interested in Art.*

CLOSE — MAX

He drops the powder into some water, stirs it, drinks, burps delicately and closes his eyes.

ADDISON'S VOICE

*The other is one to whom each production means potential ruin or fortune. This type is out to make a buck. Meet Max Fabian. He is the producer of*

ALL ABOUT EVE

*the play which has won for Eve Harrington the Sarah Siddons Award . . .*

Max rests fitfully. He twitches. A hand reaches into the SCENE, removes a bottle of Scotch from before him. The CAMERA follows the bottle to a

CLOSEUP — MARGO CHANNING

She sits at Max's left, at DeWitt's right. An attractive, strong face. She is childish, adult, reasonable, unreasonable — usually one when she should be the other, but always positive. She pours a stiff drink.

CLOSE — ADDISON

He holds out the soda bottle to her.

CLOSE — MARGO

She looks at it, and at him, as if it were a tarantula and he had gone mad.

CLOSE — ADDISON

He smiles and pours a glass of soda for himself.

ADDISON'S VOICE

*Margo Channing is a Star of the Theatre. She made her first stage appearance, at the age of four, in* Midsummer Night's Dream. *She played a fairy*

*and entered — quite unexpectedly — stark naked. She has been a Star ever since.*

CLOSE — MARGO

She sloshes her drink around moodily, pulls at it.

ADDISON'S VOICE

*Margo is a great Star. A true Star. She never was or will be anything less or anything else . . .*

(slight pause)

*. . . the part for which Eve Harrington is receiving the Sarah Siddons Award was intended originally for Margo Channing.*

CLOSE — ADDISON

Having sipped his soda water, he puts a new cigarette in his holder, leans back, lights it, looks and exhales in the general direction of the table of honor.

As he speaks the CAMERA MOVES in the direction of his glance . . .

ADDISON'S VOICE

*Having covered in tedious detail not only the history of the Sarah Siddons Society, but also the history of acting since Thespis first stepped out of the chorus line — our distinguished chairman has finally arrived at our reason for being here . . .*

At this point Addison's voice FADES OUT and the voice of the aged actor FADES IN. CAMERA is in a MEDIUM CLOSE SHOT of him and the podium.

AGED ACTOR

I have been proud and privileged to have spent my life in the Theatre — "a poor player . . . that struts and frets his hour upon the stage" — and I have been honored to be, for forty years, Chief Prompter of the Sarah Siddons Society . . .

THE SARAH SIDDONS AWARD

As the aged actor's hands lift it from its altar.

AGED ACTOR'S VOICE

Thirty-nine times have I placed in deserving hands this highest honor the Theatre knows . . .

AGED ACTOR

He grows a bit arch, he uses his eyebrows.

AGED ACTOR

Surely no actor is older than I. I have earned my place out of the sun . . .

(indulgent laughter)

. . . and never before has this Award gone to anyone younger than its recipient tonight. How fitting that it should pass from my hands to hers . . .

EVE'S HANDS

Lovely, beautifully groomed. In serene repose, they rest between a demi-tasse and an exquisite small evening bag.

AGED ACTOR'S VOICE

Such young hands. Such a young lady. Young in years, but whose heart is as old as the Theatre . . .

ADDISON

His eyes narrow quizzically as he listens. Then, slowly, he turns to look at Karen . . .

AGED ACTOR'S VOICE

Some of us are privileged to know her. We have seen beyond the beauty and artistry —

KAREN

She never ceases her thoughtful pat-a-cake with the crumbs.

AGED ACTOR'S VOICE

— that have made her name resound through the nation. We know her humility. Her devotion, her loyalty to her art.

ADDISON

His glance moves from Karen to Margo.

AGED ACTOR'S VOICE

Her love, her deep and abiding love for us —

MARGO

Her face is a mask. She looks down at the drink which she cradles with both hands.

AGED ACTOR'S VOICE

— for what we are and what we do. The Theatre. She has had one wish, one prayer, one dream. To belong to us.

AGED ACTOR

He's nearing his curtain line.

AGED ACTOR

Tonight her dream has come true. And henceforth we shall dream the same of her.

(a slight pause)

Honored members, ladies and gentlemen — for distinguished achievement in the Theatre — the Sarah Siddons Award to Miss Eve Harrington!

FULL SHOT

The entire room is galvanized into sudden and tumultuous applause. Some of the more enthusiastic gentlemen rise to their feet. Flash bulbs start popping about halfway down the table to the Aged Actor's left . . . EVE starts to rise —

CLOSE — EVE

She rises into it and the CAMERA MOVES CLOSER. Eve. Beautiful, radiant, poised, exquisitely gowned. She stands in simple and dignified response to the ovation.

HER ANGLE

A dozen photographers skip, squat and dart about like water bugs. Flash bulbs pop and pop and pop . . .

THE WAITERS

They applaud enthusiastically . . .

AGED ACTOR

Award in hand, he beams at her . . .

EVE

She smiles sweetly to her left, then to her right . . .

MAX

He's come to. He applauds lustily.

ADDISON

Applauding too — more discreetly.

MARGO

Not applauding. But you sense no deliberate slight, merely an impression that as she looks at Eve her mind is on something else . . .

KAREN

Nor is she applauding. But her gaze is similarly fixed on Eve in a strange, faraway fashion . . .

ADDISON

Still applauding, his eyes flash first at Margo and then at Karen. Then he directs them back to Eve. He smiles ever so slightly . . .

EVE

The applause has continued unabated. She turns now, and moves gracefully toward the Aged Actor, the CAMERA MOVING with her. She moves through applauding ladies and gentlemen; from below the flash bulbs keep popping . . .

As she nears her goal, the Aged Actor turns to her. He holds out the award. Her hand reaches out for it. At that PRECISE MOMENT — with the award JUST BEYOND HER FINGERTIPS — THE PICTURE HOLDS, THE ACTION STOPS. The SOUND STOPS. ADDISON'S VOICE takes over:

ADDISON'S VOICE

*Eve. Eve, the Golden Girl. The cover girl, the girl next door, the girl on the moon. . . . Time has been good to Eve. Life goes where she goes — she's been profiled, covered, revealed, reported, what she eats and when and where, what she wears and when and where, whom she knows and where she was and when and where she's going. . . .*

CLOSEUP — ADDISON

He's stopped applauding, he's sitting forward, staring intently at Eve . . . his narration continues unbroken.

ADDISON'S VOICE

*. . . Eve. You all know all about Eve. . . . what can there be to know that you don't know . . . ?*

As he leans back, the APPLAUSE FADES IN as tumultuous as before. Addison's look moves slowly from Eve to Karen.

CLOSEUP — KAREN

She leans forward now, her eyes intent on Eve. Her lovely face FILLS THE SCREEN as the APPLAUSE FADES ONCE MORE — as she thinks back:

KAREN'S VOICE

*When was it? How long? It seems a lifetime ago. Lloyd always said that in the Theatre a lifetime was a season, and a season a lifetime. It's June now. That was — early October . . . only last October. It was a drizzly night, I remember I asked the taxi to wait . . .*

Her last lines are over a —

SLOW DISSOLVE TO:

NEW YORK THEATRE STREET — NIGHT

Traffic is not heavy; the shows have broken some half-hour before. The rain is just a drizzle.

There are other theatres on the street; display lights are being extinguished. Going out just as Karen's taxi pulls up is: MARGO CHANNING in AGED IN WOOD.

CLOSER

As the taxi comes to a stop at the alley. Karen can be seen through the closed windows telling the driver to wait. Then she gets out. She takes a step, hesitates, then looks about curiously:

KAREN'S VOICE

*Where was she? Strange . . . I had become so accustomed to seeing her there night after night — I found myself looking for a girl I'd never spoken to, wondering where she was . . .*

She smiles a little at her own romanticism, puts her head down and makes her way into the alley.

ALLEY — NIGHT

CAMERA MOVING with Karen toward the stage door. She passes a recess in the theatre wall — perhaps an exit — about halfway.

EVE'S VOICE

(softly)

Mrs. Richards . . .

Karen hesitates, looks. Eve is barely distinguishable in the shadow of the recess. Karen smiles, waits. Eve comes out. A gooseneck light above them reveals her . . .

She wears a cheap trench coat, low-heeled shoes, a rain hat stuck on the back of her head . . . her large, luminous eyes seem to glow up at Karen in the strange half-light.

KAREN

So there you are. It seemed odd, suddenly, your not being there . . .

EVE

Why should you think I wouldn't be?

KAREN

Why should you be? After all, six nights a week — for weeks — of watching even Margo Channing enter and leave a theatre —

EVE

I hope you don't mind my speaking to you . . .

KAREN

Not at all.

EVE

I've seen you so often — it took every bit of courage I could raise —

KAREN

(smiles)

To speak to just a playwright's wife? I'm the lowest form of celebrity.

EVE

You're Margo Channing's best friend. You and your husband are always with her — and Mr. Sampson . . . what's he like?

KAREN

(grins)

Bill Sampson? He's — he's a director.

EVE

He's the best.

KAREN

He'll agree with you. Tell me — what do you do between the time Margo goes in and comes out? Just huddle in that doorway and wait?

EVE

Oh, no. I see the play.

KAREN

(incredulous)

You see the play? You've seen the play every performance?

Eve nods)

But, don't you find it — I mean apart from everything else — don't you find it expensive?

EVE

Standing room doesn't cost much. I manage.

Karen contemplates Eve. Then she takes her arm.

KAREN

I'm going to take you to Margo . . .

EVE

(hanging back)

Oh, no . . .

KAREN

She's got to meet you —

EVE

No, I'd be imposing on her, I'd be just another tongue-tied gushing fan . . .

Karen practically propels her toward the stage door.

KAREN

(insisting)

There isn't another like you, there couldn't be —

EVE

But if I'd known . . . maybe some other time . . . I mean, looking like this . . .

KAREN

You look just fine . . .

(they're at the stage door)

. . . by the way. What's your name?

EVE

Eve. Eve Harrington.

Karen opens the door. They go in.

BACKSTAGE — NIGHT

Everything, including the doorman, looks fireproof.

Eve enters like a novitiate's first visit to the Vatican. Karen, with a "Good evening, Gus —" to the doorman, leads the way toward Margo's stage dressing room. Eve, drinking in the wonderment of all she surveys, lags behind. Karen waits for her to catch up . . .

EVE

You can breathe it — can't you? Like some magic perfume . . .

Karen smiles, takes Eve's arm. They proceed to Margo's dressing room.

OUTSIDE MARGO'S DRESSING ROOM

No star on the closed door; the paint is peeling. A typewritten chit, thumbtacked, says MISS CHANNING.

As Karen and Eve approach it, an uninhibited guffaw from Margo makes them pause.

KAREN

(whispers)

You wait a minute . . .

(she smiles)

. . . now don't run away —

Eve smiles shakily. At the same moment:

MARGO'S VOICE

(loudly — through the door)

"Honey chile," I said, "if the South had won the war, you could write the same plays about the North!"

Karen enters during the line.

MARGO'S DRESSING ROOM — NIGHT

It is a medium-sized box, lined with hot-water pipes and

cracked plaster. It is furnished in beat-up wicker. A door leads to an old-fashioned bathroom.

Margo is at the dressing table. She wears an old wrapper, her hair drawn back tightly to fit under the wig which lies before her like a dead poodle. Also before her is an almost finished drink.

LLOYD RICHARDS is stretched out on the wicker chaise. He's in his late thirties, sensitive, literate.

Between them, by the dressing table, is BIRDIE — Margo's maid. Her age is unimportant. She was conceived during a split week in Walla Walla and born in a carnival riot. She is fiercely loyal to Margo.

Karen enters during the line Margo started while she was outside. Lloyd chuckles, Birdie cackles.

KAREN

Hi.

(she goes to kiss Lloyd)

Hello, darling —

LLOYD

How was the concert?

KAREN

Loud.

MARGO

Hi.

(she goes right on — in a thick "Suth'n" accent)

"Well, now, Mis' Channin', ah don't think you can rightly say we lost the wah, we was mo'

BIRDIE

Lemme fix you a drink.

KAREN

No, thanks, Birdie.

stahved out, you might say — an' that's what ah don' unnerstand about all these plays about sex-stahved Suth'n women — sex is one thing we was nevah stahved for in the South!"

Karen laughs with them.

LLOYD

Margo's interview with a lady reporter from the South —

BIRDIE

The minute it gets printed they're gonna fire on Gettysburg all over again . . .

MARGO

It was Fort Sumter they fired on —

BIRDIE

I never played Fort Sumter.

She takes the wig into the bathroom. Margo starts creaming the makeup off her face.

MARGO

Honey chile had a point. You know, I can remember plays about women — even from the South — where it never even occurred to them whether they wanted to marry their fathers more than their brothers . . .

LLOYD

That was way back . . .

MARGO

Within your time, buster. Lloyd, honey, be a playwright with guts. Write me one about a nice, normal woman who shoots her husband.

Birdie comes out of the bathroom without the wig.

BIRDIE

You need new girdles.

MARGO

Buy some.

BIRDIE

The same size?

MARGO

Of course!

BIRDIE

Well. I guess a real tight girdle helps when you're playin' a lunatic.

She picks up Lloyd's empty glass, asks "more?" He shakes his head. She pours herself a quick one.

KAREN

(firmly)

Margo does not play a lunatic, Birdie.

BIRDIE

I know. She just keeps hearin' her dead father play a banjo.

MARGO

It's the tight girdle that does it.

KAREN

I find these wisecracks increasingly less funny! *Aged in Wood* happens to be a fine and distinguished play —

LLOYD

— 'at's my loyal little woman.

KAREN

The critics thought so, the audiences certainly think so — packed houses, tickets four months in advance — I can't see that either of Lloyd's last two plays have hurt you any!

LLOYD

Easy, now . . .

MARGO

(grins)
Relax, kid. It's only me and my big mouth . . .

KAREN

(mollified)
It's just that you get me so mad sometimes . . . of all the women in the world with nothing to complain about —

MARGO

(dryly)
Ain't it the truth?

KAREN

Yes, it is! You're talented, famous, wealthy — people waiting around night after night just to see you, even in the wind and rain . . .

MARGO

Autograph fiends! They're not people — those little beasts who run in packs like coyotes —

KAREN

They're your fans, your audience —

MARGO

They're nobody's fans! They're juvenile delinquents, mental defectives, they're nobody's audience, they never see a play or a movie, even — they're never indoors long enough!

There is a pause. Lloyd applauds lightly.

KAREN

Well . . . there's one indoors now. I've brought her back to see you.

MARGO

You've *what?*

KAREN

(in a whisper)

She's just outside the door.

MARGO

(to Birdie — also a whisper)

The heave-ho.

Birdie starts. Karen stops her. It's all in whispers, now, until Eve comes in.

KAREN

You can't put her out, I promised . . . Margo, you've got to see her, she worships you, it's like something out of a book —

LLOYD

That book is out of print, Karen, those days are gone. Fans no longer pull the carriage through the streets — they tear off clothes and steal wrist watches . . .

KAREN

If you'd only see her, you're her whole life — you must have spotted her by now, she's always there . . .

MARGO

Kind of mousy trench coat and funny hat?

(Karen nods)

How could I miss her? Every night and matinee — well . . .

Karen goes to the door, opens it. Eve comes in. Karen closes the door behind her. A moment.

EVE

(simply)

I thought you'd forgotten about me.

KAREN

Not at all.

(her arm through Eve's)

Margo, this is Eve Harrington.

Margo changes swiftly into a first-lady-of-the-theatre manner.

MARGO

(musically)

How do you do, my dear?

BIRDIE

(mutters)

Oh, brother.

EVE

Hello, Miss Channing.

KAREN

My husband . . .

LLOYD

(nicely)

Hello, Miss Harrington.

EVE

How do you do, Mr. Richards?

MARGO

(graciously)

And this is my good friend and companion, Miss Birdie Coonan.

BIRDIE

Oh, brother.

EVE

Miss Coonan . . .

LLOYD

(to Birdie)

Oh, brother what?

BIRDIE

When she gets like this . . . all of a sudden she's playin' Hamlet's mother.

MARGO

(quiet menace)

I'm sure you must have things to do in the bathroom, Birdie dear.

BIRDIE

If I haven't, I'll find something till you're normal.

She goes into the bathroom.

MARGO

Dear Birdie. Won't you sit down, Miss Worthington?

KAREN

Harrington.

MARGO

I'm so sorry . . . Harrington. Won't you sit down?

EVE

Thank you.

She sits. A short lull.

| MARGO | KAREN |
| --- | --- |
| Would you like a drink? It's right beside you . . . | I was telling Margo and Lloyd about how often you'd seen the play . . . |

They start together, and stop in deference to each other. They're a little flustered. But not Eve.

EVE

(to Margo)

No, thank you.

(to Lloyd)

Yes. I've seen every performance.

LLOYD

(delighted)

Every performance? Then — am I safe in assuming you like it?

EVE

I'd like anything Miss Channing played . . .

MARGO

(beams)

Would you, really? How sweet —

LLOYD

(flatly)

I doubt very much that you'd like her in *The Hairy Ape*.

EVE

Please don't misunderstand me, Mr. Richards. I think that part of Miss Channing's greatness lies in her ability to choose the best plays —

MARGO

(sighs)

And there's so little to choose from these days . . .

KAREN

(warningly)

Margo . . .

LLOYD

And then there's always the playwright's problem — whom can we borrow from Hollywood to play it?

MARGO

(icily)

I understand that Hopalong Cassidy is looking for something.

EVE

(deftly averting the squall)

Your new play is for Miss Channing, isn't it, Mr. Richards?

MARGO

Of course it is.

LLOYD

How'd you hear about it?

EVE

There was an item in the *Times*. I like the title. *Footsteps on the Ceiling*.

LLOYD

Let's get back to this one. Have you really seen every performance?

(Eve nods)

Why? I'm curious.

Eve looks at Margo, then drops her eyes.

EVE

Well. If I didn't come to see the play, I wouldn't have anywhere else to go.

MARGO

There are other plays . . .

EVE

Not with you in them. Not by Mr. Richards . . .

LLOYD

But you must have friends, a family, a home —

Eve pauses. Then shakes her head.

KAREN

Tell us about it — Eve.

Eve looks at her — grateful because Karen called her "Eve." Then away, again . . .

EVE

If I only knew how . . .

KAREN

Try . . .

EVE

Well . . .

Birdie comes out of the bathroom. Everybody looks at her sharply. She realizes she's in on something important. She closes the door quietly, leans against it.

EVE

Well . . . it started with the play before this one.

LLOYD

*Remembrance.*

EVE

(nods)

*Remembrance.*

MARGO

Did you see it here in New York?

EVE

San Francisco. It was the last week. I went one night . . . the most important night of my life — until this one. Anyway . . . I found myself going the next night — and the next and the next. Every performance. Then, when the show went East — I went East.

BIRDIE

I'll never forget that blizzard the night we played Cheyenne. A cold night. First time I ever saw a brassiere break like a piece of matzo.

Eve looks up at her unsmilingly, then back to her hands.

KAREN

Eve . . . why don't you start at the beginning?

EVE

It couldn't possibly interest you.

MARGO

Please . . .

Eve speaks simply and without self-pity:

EVE

I guess it started back home. Wisconsin, that is. There was just Mum and Dad — and me. I was the only child, and I made believe a lot when I was a kid — I acted out all sorts of things . . .

what they were isn't important. But somehow acting and make-believe began to fill up my life more and more. It got so that I couldn't tell the real from the unreal except that the unreal seemed more real to me . . . I'm talking a lot of gibberish, aren't I?

LLOYD

Not at all . . .

EVE

Farmers were poor in those days, that's what Dad was — a farmer. I had to help out. So I quit school and I went to Milwaukee. I became a secretary. In a brewery.

(she smiles)

When you're a secretary in a brewery — it's pretty hard to make believe you're anything else. Everything is beer. It wasn't much fun, but it helped at home — and there was a Little Theatre group . . . like a drop of rain on a desert. That's where I met Eddie. He was a radio technician. We played *Liliom* for three performances, I was awful — then the war came, and we got married. Eddie was in the Air Force — and they sent him to the South Pacific. You were with the O.W.I., weren't you, Mr. Richards?

(Lloyd nods)

That's what *Who's Who* says . . . well, with Eddie gone, my life went back to beer. Except for a letter a week. One week Eddie wrote he had a leave coming up. I'd saved my money and vacation time. I went to San Francisco to meet him.

(a slight pause)

Eddie wasn't there. They forwarded the telegram from Milwaukee — the one that came from Washington to say that Eddie wasn't coming at all. That Eddie was dead . . .

(Karen puts her hand on Lloyd's)

. . . so I figured I'd stay in San Francisco. I was alone, but I couldn't go back without Eddie. I found a job. And his insurance helped . . . and there were theatres in San Francisco. And one night Margo Channing came to play in *Remembrance* . . . and I went to see it. And — well — here I am . . .

She finishes dry-eyed and self-composed. Margo squeezes the bridge of her nose, dabs at her eyes.

BIRDIE

(finally)

What a story! Everything but the bloodhounds snappin' at her rear end.

That breaks the spell. Margo turns on her —

MARGO

There are some human experiences, Birdie, that do not take place in a vaudeville house — and that even a fifth-rate vaudevillian should understand and respect!

(to Eve)

I want to apologize for Birdie's —

BIRDIE

(snaps in)

You don't have to apologize for me!

(to Eve)

I'm sorry if I hurt your feelings. It's just my way of talkin' . . .

EVE

(nicely)

You didn't hurt my feelings, Miss Coonan.

BIRDIE

Call me Birdie.

(to Margo)

As for bein' fifth rate — I closed the first half for eleven years an' you know it!

She slams into the bathroom again. At that precise instant BILL SAMPSON flings open the door to the dressing room. He's youngish, vital, undisciplined. He lugs a beat-up suitcase which he drops as he crosses to Margo —

BILL

Forty-seven minutes from now my plane takes off and how do I find you? Not ready yet, looking like a junk yard —

MARGO

Thank you so much.

BILL

Is it sabotage, does my career mean nothing to you? Have you no human consideration?

MARGO

Show me a human and I might have!

KAREN

(conscious of Eve)

Bill . . .

BILL

The airlines have clocks, even if you haven't! I start shooting a week from Monday — Zanuck is impatient, he wants me, he needs me!

KAREN

(louder)

Bill —

MARGO

Zanuck, Zanuck, Zanuck! What are you two — lovers?

Bill grins suddenly, drops to one knee beside her.

BILL

Only in some ways. You're prettier . . .

MARGO

I'm a junk yard.

KAREN

(yells)

Bill!

BILL

(vaguely — to Karen)

Huh?

KAREN

This is Eve Harrington.

Bill flashes a fleeting look at Eve.

BILL

Hi.

(to Margo)

My wonderful junk yard. The mystery and dreams you find in a junk yard —

MARGO

(kisses him)

I love a psychotic.

Bill grins, rises, sees Eve as if for the first time.

BILL

Hello, what's your name?

EVE

Eve. Eve Harrington.

KAREN

You've already met.

BILL

Where?

KAREN

Right here. A minute ago.

BILL

That's nice.

MARGO

She, too, is a great admirer of yours.

BIRDIE

Imagine. All this admiration in just one room.

BILL

You. Take your mistress into the bathroom and dress her.

(Birdie opens her mouth)

Without comment.

Birdie shuts it and goes into the bathroom. In a moment we hear a shower start to run. Eve gets up.

KAREN

You're not going, are you?

EVE

I think I'd better. It's been — well, I can hardly find the words to say how it's been . . .

MARGO

(rises)

No, don't go . . .

EVE

The four of you must have so much to say to each other — with Mr. Sampson leaving . . .

Margo, impulsively, crosses to Eve.

MARGO

Stick around. Please. Tell you what — we'll put Stanislavsky on his plane, you and I, then go somewhere and talk.

EVE

Well — if I'm not in the way . . .

MARGO

I won't be a minute.

She darts into the bathroom. Eve sits down again.

KAREN

Lloyd, we've *got* to go —

Lloyd gets up. Karen crosses to pound on the bathroom door. She yells — the shower is going . . .

KAREN

Margo, good night! I'll call you tomorrow!

Margo's answer is lost in the shower noise. Karen crosses to kiss Bill. She's joined by Lloyd.

KAREN

Good luck, genius . . .

BILL

Geniuses don't need good luck.

(he grins)

I do.

LLOYD

I'm not worried about you.

BILL

Keep the thought.

They shake hands warmly. Karen and Lloyd move to Eve.

KAREN

Good night, Eve. I hope I see you again, soon —

EVE

I'll be at the old stand, tomorrow matinee —

KAREN

Not just that way. As a friend.

EVE

I'd like that.

LLOYD

It's been a real pleasure, Eve.

EVE

I hope so, Mr. Richards. Good night.

Lloyd shakes her hand, crosses to join Karen who waits at the open dressing-room door.

EVE

Mrs. Richards . . .
(Karen and Lloyd look back)
I'll never forget this night as long as I live. And I'll never forget you for making it possible . . .

Karen smiles warmly. She closes the door. They leave.

BACKSTAGE

CAMERA PANS Karen and Lloyd as they cross toward the stage door.

KAREN'S VOICE

*— and I'll never forget you, Eve. Where were we going that night, Lloyd and I? Funny, the things you remember — and the things you don't . . .*

MARGO'S DRESSING ROOM — NIGHT

Eve sits on the same chair. Bill keeps moving around. Eve never takes her eyes off him. He offers her a cigarette. She shakes her head. He looks at his watch.

EVE

You said forty-seven minutes. You'll never make it.

BILL

(grins)

I told a lie. We'll make it easily. Margo's got no more conception of time than a halibut.

He sprawls on the chaise, closes his eyes. A pause.

EVE

(finally)

So you're going to Hollywood.

Bill grunts in the affirmative. Silence.

BILL

Why?

EVE

I just wondered.

BILL

Just wondered what?

EVE

Why.

BILL

Why what?

EVE

Why you have to go out there.

BILL

I don't have to. I want to.

EVE

Is it the money?

BILL

Eighty per cent of it will go for taxes.

EVE

Then why? Why, if you're the best and most successful young director in the theatre —

BILL

The Theatuh, the Theatuh —

(he sits up)

— what book of rules says the Theatre exists only within some ugly buildings crowded into one square mile of New York City? Or London, Paris or Vienna?

(he gets up)

Listen, junior. And learn. Want to know what the Theatre is? A flea circus. Also opera. Also rodeos, carnivals, ballets, Indian tribal dances, Punch and Judy, a one-man band — all Theatre. Wherever there's magic and make-believe and an audience — there's Theatre. Donald Duck, Ibsen and The Lone Ranger. Sarah Bernhardt, Poodles Hanneford, Lunt and Fontanne, Betty Grable — Rex the Wild Horse and Eleanora Duse. You don't understand them all, you don't like them all — why should you? The Theatre's for everybody — you included, but not exclusively — so don't approve or disapprove. It may not be your Theatre, but it's Theatre for somebody, somewhere . . .

EVE

I just asked a simple question.

BILL

(grins)

And I shot my mouth off. Nothing personal, junior, no offense . . .

(he sits back down)

. . . it's just that there's so much bushwah in this Ivory Green Room they call the Theatuh — sometimes it gets up around my chin . . .

He lies down again.

EVE

But Hollywood. You mustn't stay there.

BILL

(he closes his eyes)

It's only a one-picture deal.

EVE

So few come back . . .

BILL

Yeah. They keep you under drugs out there with armed guards . . .

A pause.

EVE

I read George Jean Nathan every week.

BILL

Also Addison DeWitt.

EVE

Every day.

BILL

You didn't have to tell me.

Margo, putting on an earring, buzzes out of the bathroom followed by Birdie. Bill sits up.

MARGO

(en route)

I understand it's the latest thing — just one earring. If it isn't, it's going to be — I can't find the other . . .

She grabs her pocketbook, starts rummaging. Out comes a letter.

BILL

Throw that dreary thing away, it bores me —

Margo drops it in the wastebasket, keeps rummaging.

EVE

(concerned)

Where do you suppose it could be?

BIRDIE

It'll show up.

MARGO

(gives up)

Oh, well . . .

(to Birdie)

. . . look through the wigs, maybe it got caught —

BILL

Real diamonds in a wig. The world we live in.

MARGO

(she's been looking)

Where's my coat?

BIRDIE

Right where you left it . . .

She goes behind the chaise. She comes up with a magnificent mink.

BILL

(to Margo)

The seams.

Margo starts to straighten them.

MARGO

(to Eve)

Can't keep his eyes off my legs.

BILL

Like a nylon lemon peel —

MARGO

(straightens up)

Byron couldn't have said it more graciously. Here we go —

By now she's in the coat and has Eve's arm, heading for the door. Bill puts his arms around Birdie.

BILL

Got any messages? What do you want me to tell Tyrone Power?

BIRDIE

Just give him my phone number. I'll tell him myself.

Bill kisses her cheek. She kisses Bill.

BIRDIE

Kill the people.

(to Margo)

Got your key?

MARGO

(nods)

See you home . . .

Margo and Eve precede Bill out of the door.

DISSOLVE TO:

LA GUARDIA FIELD — NIGHT

Baggage counter. The rain has stopped, but it's wet.

Margo, Eve and Bill are stymied behind two or three couples waiting to be checked in. Margo's arm is through Bill's. They become increasingly aware of their imminent separation. Eve senses her superfluity.

A lull. Bill cranes at the passenger heading the line, in earnest conversation with the dispatcher. He sighs.

MARGO

They have to time it so everybody gets on at the last minute. So they can close the doors and let you sit.

The man up ahead moves on.

BILL

Ah . . .

EVE

I have a suggestion.

(they look at her)

There's really not much time left — I mean, you haven't had a minute alone yet, and — well, I could take care of everything here and meet you at the gate with the ticket . . . if you'd like.

BILL

I think we'd like very much. Sure you won't mind?

EVE

Of course not.

Bill hands Eve the ticket. Margo smiles gratefully at her. Eve smiles back.

PASSAGE AND GATE — LA GUARDIA — NIGHT

It's covered, with glass windows. CAMERA TRUCKS BEFORE Margo and Bill. Her arm in his.

BILL

She's quite a girl, this what's-her-name . . .

MARGO

Eve. I'd forgotten they grew that way . . .

BILL

That lack of pretense, that sort of strange directness and understanding —

MARGO

Did she tell you about the Theatre and what it meant?

BILL

(grins)

I told her. I sounded off.

MARGO

All the religions in the world rolled into one, and we're gods and goddesses . . . isn't it silly, suddenly I've developed a big, protective feeling for her — a lamb loose in our big stone jungle.

Bill pulls her to one side. Some passengers go by . . . the CAMERA MOVES IN. A pause.

MARGO

Take care of yourself out there.

BILL

I understand they've got the Indians pretty well in hand.

MARGO

Bill . . .

BILL

Huh?

MARGO

Don't get stuck on some glamour puss —

BILL

I'll try.

MARGO

You're not such a bargain, you know, conceited and thoughtless and messy —

BILL

Everybody can't be Gregory Peck.

MARGO

You're a setup for some gorgeous wide-eyed young babe.

BILL

How childish are you going to get before you quit it?

MARGO

I don't want to be childish, I'd settle for just a few years —

BILL

(firmly)

And cut that out right now.

MARGO

Am I going to lose you, Bill? Am I?

BILL

As of this moment you're six years old . . .

He starts to kiss her, stops when he becomes aware of Eve standing near them. She has his ticket in her hand.

EVE

All ready.

She hands Bill his ticket, they start toward the gate.

BOARDING GATE — LA GUARDIA — NIGHT

A few visitors. Bill hands his ticket to the guard, turns to Eve.

BILL

Thanks for your help . . . good luck.

EVE

Good-bye, Mr. Sampson.

Bill puts his arms around Margo.

BILL

Knit me a muffler.

MARGO

Call me when you get in . . .

They kiss. Margo's arms tighten desperately. Bill pulls away, kisses her again lightly, starts for the plane. Margo turns away. Eve puts her arm through Margo's.

Bill pauses en route to the plane.

BILL

Hey — junior . . .

Margo turns to look at him with Eve.

BILL

Keep your eye on her. Don't let her get lonely. She's a loose lamb in a jungle . . .

Eve looks at Margo. Margo smiles.

EVE

Don't worry . . .

Bill waves, climbs aboard. The door is closed behind him, the departure routine starts.

Margo and Eve turn to go. They walk away from CAMERA down the PASSAGE. As they walk, Eve gently disengages her arm from Margo's and puts it comfortingly about her.

MARGO'S VOICE

*That same night we sent for Eve's things, her few pitiful possessions . . . she moved into the little guest room on the top floor . . . she cried when she saw it — it was so like her little room back home in Wisconsin.*

*The next three weeks were out of a fairly tale — and I was Cinderella in the last act. Eve became my sister, lawyer, mother, friend, psychiatrist and cop — the honeymoon was on . . .*

SLOW DISSOLVE TO:

MARGO'S LIVING ROOM — DAY

It's one floor above street level. A long narrow room, smartly furnished — including a Sarah Siddons Award.

MARGO'S NARRATIVE continues over this scene which is a SILENT ONE.

Eve sits at a smart desk. She is just arranging a stack of letters which she carries to Margo with a pen. Margo sits comfortably by the fire with a play script. She hands the script up to Eve, shakes her head and holds her nose. Eve smiles, takes the script, hands Margo the letters to sign.

Birdie comes in with a tea tray which she sets on a low table before the fire.

The phone rings.

Birdie and Eve both go for it. Eve gets there first. By her polite but negative attitude, we know she is giving someone a skillful brush-off.

Birdie glares first at her, then at Margo.

Margo leans her head back, closes her eyes blissfully . . .

Birdie slams the double door to the landing on her way out.

DISSOLVE TO:

THEATRE — BACKSTAGE

From the wings. The audience is NEVER VISIBLE. Eve in the foreground, her back to CAMERA. Margo and company taking a curtain call. Tumultuous applause . . . the curtain falls. The cast, except for Margo and two male leads, walks off. The curtain rises again . . .

CLOSE — EVE

Watching and listening to the storm of applause. Her eyes shine, she clasps and unclasps her hands . . .

THE STAGE

Eve again in the foreground, but CLOSER. Again the curtain falls. This time the two men go off. Curtain rises on Margo alone. If anything, the applause builds . . .

CLOSEUP — EVE

That same hypnotic look . . . there are tears in her eyes. The curtain falls offscene, then rises again —

CLOSE — MARGO

The curtain falls again between her and CAMERA . . .

BACKSTAGE

The curtain just settling on the floor. Margo starts off.

STAGE MANAGER

One more?

MARGO

(shakes her head)

From now on it's not applause — it's just something to do till the aisles get less crowded.

She walks as she talks and winds up at Eve — still in the wings. Eve's eyes are wet, she dabs at her nose.

MARGO

What — again?

EVE

I could watch you play that last scene a thousand times and cry every time —

MARGO

(grins)

Performance number one thousand of this one —

if I play it that long — will take place in a well-padded booby hatch.

She takes Eve's arm, they stroll toward her dressing room.

EVE

I must say you can certainly tell Mr. Sampson's been gone a month.

MARGO

You certainly can. Especially if you're me between now and tomorrow morning.

EVE

I mean the performance. Except for you, you'd think he'd never even directed it — it's disgraceful the way they change everything around.

MARGO

(smiles)

Well, teacher's away and actors will be actors.

EVE

During your second act scene with your father, Roger Ferraday's supposed to stay way upstage at the arch. He's been coming closer down every night.

MARGO

When he gets too close, I'll spit in his eye.

They're at her dressing room by now. Margo's been unhooking her gown, with Eve's help. They go in.

MARGO'S DRESSING ROOM — NIGHT

It's undergone quite a change. A new carpet, chintz covers for the furniture, new lampshades, dainty curtains across the filthy barred window.

Birdie waits within.

MARGO

(entering)

You bought the new girdles a size smaller. I can feel it.

BIRDIE

Something maybe grew a size larger.

MARGO

When we get home you're going to get into one of those girdles and act for two and a half hours.

BIRDIE

I couldn't get into the girdle in two an' a half hours.

Margo's out of her wig and dress by now. She gets into her robe, sits at the dressing table. Eve's on the chaise, by the discarded costume.

EVE

You haven't noticed my latest bit of interior decorating.

MARGO

(turns, looks)

Well, you've done so much . . . what's new?

EVE

The curtains. I made them myself.

MARGO

They are lovely. Aren't they lovely, Birdie?

BIRDIE

Adorable. We now got everything a dressing room needs except a basketball hoop.

MARGO

Just because you can't even work a zipper. It was very thoughtful, Eve, and I appreciate it —

A pause. Eve rises, picking up Margo's costume.

EVE

While you're cleaning up, I'll take this to the wardrobe mistress —

MARGO

Don't bother. Mrs. Brown'll be along for it in a minute.

EVE

No trouble at all.

And she goes out with the costume. Birdie opens her mouth, shuts it, then opens it again.

BIRDIE

If I may be so bold as to say something — did you ever hear the word "union"?

MARGO

Behind in your dues? How much?

BIRDIE

I haven't got a union. I'm slave labor.

MARGO

Well?

BIRDIE

But the wardrobe women have got one. And next to a tenor, a wardrobe woman is the touchiest thing in show business —

MARGO

(catching on)

Oh-oh.

BIRDIE

She's got two things to do — carry clothes an'

press 'em wrong — an' just let anybody else muscle in . . .

MARGO

(remembering)

Detroit.

(she jumps up)

Detroit! When you took that stain out — they nearly closed us . . .

She hurries to the door and out after Eve.

BACKSTAGE — OUTSIDE MARGO'S DRESSING ROOM

Margo pops out, looks for Eve, then stares in amazement:

EVE

Near the wings. She stands before a couple of cheval mirrors set up for cast members. She has Margo's dress held up against her body. She turns this way and that, bows as if to applause — mimicking Margo exactly.

MARGO

She watches her curiously. Then she smiles.

MARGO

(calling)

Eve —

EVE

Startled, she whips the gown away, turns to Margo . . .

MARGO

Smiles understandingly.

MARGO

(quietly)

I think we'd better let Mrs. Brown pick up the wardrobe . . .

Wordlessly, Eve brings it toward her . . .

DISSOLVE TO:

MARGO'S BEDROOM — NIGHT

Margo's asleep. A bedside clock with a luminous dial reads 3 A.M. exactly. The phone rings. Her head comes up out of the pillow, she shakes it. She fumbles, switches on a lamp, then picks up the phone.

MARGO

Hello . . .

OPERATOR'S VOICE

We are ready with your call to Beverly Hills . . .

MARGO

Call, what call?

OPERATOR'S VOICE

Is this Templeton 8-9970? Miss Margo Channing?

MARGO

That's right, but I don't understand —

OPERATOR'S VOICE

We are ready with the call you placed for 12 midnight, California time, to Mr. William Sampson in Beverly Hills . . .

MARGO

*I* placed . . . ?

OPERATOR'S VOICE

Go ahead, please . . .

BILL'S VOICE

(a loud, happy squawk)

Margo! What a wonderful surprise!

Margo jumps at his vehemence. BILL, when we reveal him during the scene, is also in bed. His clock says midnight.

BILL

(continuing)

What a thoughtful, ever-lovin' thing to do —

MARGO

(dazed)

Bill? Have I gone crazy, Bill?

BILL

You're my girl, aren't you?

MARGO

That I am . . .

BILL

Then you're crazy.

MARGO

(nods in agreement)

When — when are you coming back?

BILL

I leave in a week — the picture's all wrapped up, we previewed last night . . . those previews. Like opening out of town, but terrifying. There's nothing you can do, you're trapped, you're in a tin can —

MARGO

— in a tin can, cellophane or wrapped in a Navajo blanket, I want you home . . .

BILL

You in a hurry?

MARGO

A big hurry, be quick about it — so good night, darling, and sleep tight . . .

BILL

Wait a minute! You can't hang up, you haven't even said it —

MARGO

Bill, you know how much I do — but over the phone, now really, that's kid stuff . . .

BILL

Kid stuff or not, it doesn't happen every day, I want to hear it — and if you won't say it, you can sing it . . .

MARGO

(convinced she's gone mad)

*Sing* it?

BILL

Sure! Like the Western Union boys used to do . . .

Margo's eyes pop. Her jaw and the phone sag . . .

MARGO

Bill . . . Bill, it's your birthday.

BILL

And who remembered it? Who was there on the dot, at twelve midnight . . . ?

Margo knows damn well it wasn't she.

MARGO

(miserably)
Happy birthday, darling . . .

BILL

The reading could have been better, but you said it — now "many happy returns of the day . . ."

MARGO

(the same)
Many happy returns of the day . . .

BILL

I get a party, don't I?

MARGO

Of course, birthday and welcome home . . . Who'll I ask?

BILL

(laughs)
It's no secret, I know all about the party — Eve wrote me . . .

MARGO

She did . . . ?

BILL

She hasn't missed a week since I left — but you know all that, you probably tell her what to write

. . . anyway, I sent her a list of people to ask — check with her.

MARGO

Yeah . . . I will.

BILL

How is Eve? Okay?

MARGO

Okay.

BILL

I love you . . .

MARGO

(mutters)

I'll check with Eve . . .

BILL

What?

MARGO

I love you, too. Good night, darling —

BILL

See you . . .

Margo hangs up. Bill hangs up. He replaces his phone, picks up his book.

Margo puts her phone away. She gets a cigarette. She lights it. She rolls over on her back . . .

DISSOLVE TO:

MARGO'S BEDROOM — DAY

Margo is propped up in bed, still reflective. Birdie comes in with her breakfast tray and a "Hi" which gets a "Hi" from Margo. She starts on some petty chores. Margo takes a sip of orange juice . . .

MARGO

Birdie —

BIRDIE

Hmm?

MARGO

You don't like Eve, do you?

BIRDIE

Do you want an argument or an answer?

MARGO

An answer.

BIRDIE

No.

MARGO

Why not?

BIRDIE

Now you want an argument.

MARGO

She works hard.

BIRDIE

Night an' day.

MARGO

She's loyal and efficient —

BIRDIE

Like an agent with one client.

MARGO

She thinks only of me . . .

(no answer from Birdie)

. . . doesn't she?

BIRDIE

(finally)

Well . . . let's say she thinks only *about* you, anyway . . .

MARGO

How do you mean that?

Birdie stops whatever it is she's doing.

BIRDIE

I'll tell you how. Like — let's see — like she was

studyin' you, like you were a play or a book or a set of blueprints. How you walk, talk, think, eat, sleep —

MARGO

(breaks in; sharply)

I'm sure that's very flattering, Birdie, and I'm sure there's nothing wrong with it!

There's a sharp, brisk knock. Eve comes in. She's dressed in a smart suit. She carries a leather portfolio.

EVE

Good morning!

Margo says "Good morning," Birdie says nothing. Eve shows off the suit, proudly.

EVE

Well — what do you think of my elegant new suit?

MARGO

Very becoming. It looks better on you than it did on me.

EVE

(scoffs)

I can imagine. You know, all it needed was some taking in here and letting out there — are you sure you won't want it yourself?

MARGO

Quite sure. I find it just a bit too — too "Seventeenish" for me . . .

EVE

(laughs)

Oh, come now, as though you were an old lady . . . I'm on my way. Is there anything more you've thought of — ?

MARGO

There's the script to go back to the Guild —

EVE

I've got it.

MARGO

— and those checks or whatever it is for the income-tax man.

EVE

Right here.

MARGO

It seems I can't think of a thing you haven't thought of . . .

EVE

(smiles)

That's my job.

(she turns to go)

See you at tea time . . .

MARGO

Eve . . .

(Eve turns at the door)

. . . by any chance, did you place a call from me to Bill for midnight California time?

EVE

(gasps)

Oh, golly. And I forgot to tell you —

MARGO

Yes, dear. You forgot all about it.

EVE

Well, I was sure you'd want to, of course, being his birthday, and you've been so busy these past few days, and last night I meant to tell you before you went out with the Richards — and I guess I was asleep when you got home . . .

MARGO

Yes, I guess you were. It — it was very thoughtful of you, Eve.

EVE

Mr. Sampson's birthday. I certainly wouldn't forget that. You'd never forgive me.

(she smiles shyly)

As a matter of fact, I sent him a telegram myself . . .

And she's gone. Margo stares at the closed door. Then at Birdie. Birdie, without comment, goes out. Margo, alone, looks down at her orange juice. Absently, she twirls it in its bed of shaved ice . . .

SLOW DISSOLVE TO:

MARGO'S BEDROOM — NIGHT

It's January. The night of Margo's party for Bill. Margo is all dressed except for jewelry. She stands before her dressing table putting it on. She sips at an enormous Martini . . .

MARGO'S VOICE

*Bill's welcome-home-birthday party . . . a night to go down in history. Like the Chicago fire — or the Massacre of the Huguenots. Even before the party started, I could smell disaster in the air . . . I knew it, I sensed it even as I finished dressing for that blasted party . . .*

Birdie comes in.

BIRDIE

You all put together?

MARGO

My back's open.

(Birdie goes to work on it)

Did the extra help get here?

BIRDIE

There's some loose characters dressed like maids and butlers. Who'd you call — the William Morris Agency?

MARGO

You're not being funny. I could get actors for less. What about the food?

BIRDIE

The caterer had to go back for the hors d'oeuvres —

(she zips Margo)

Voilà.

MARGO

(laughs)

That French ventriloquist taught you a lot, didn't he?

BIRDIE

There was nothing he didn't know.

(she starts tidying the room)

There's a message from the bartender. Does Miss Channing know she ordered domestic gin by mistake?

MARGO

The only thing I ordered by mistake is the guests.

(Birdie cackles)

They're domestic, too, and they don't care what

they drink as long as it burns. Where's Bill? He's late.

BIRDIE

Late for what?

MARGO

Don't be dense. The party.

BIRDIE

I ain't dense. And he's been here twenty minutes.

MARGO

Well, I certainly think it's odd he hasn't even come up . . .

Her glance meets Birdie's. She turns and strolls out.

THIRD FLOOR LANDING — NIGHT

Margo speeds up going down the steps.

SECOND FLOOR LANDING — NIGHT

Margo slows up again deliberately as she reaches the landing. Sound of Bill and Eve laughing together from the living room. Margo strolls toward it casually as the CAMERA PANS with her.

We see Eve seated, looking up fascinatedly at Bill as he talks. Out of the laughter . . .

BILL

"Don't let it worry you," said the cameraman,

"Even DeMille couldn't see anything looking through the wrong end —"

(Eve chuckles)

So that was the first and last time —

Eve sees Margo approach. She gets up. Bill turns.

MARGO'S LIVING ROOM — NIGHT

As Margo strolls up, very off-hand.

MARGO

(casually)

Don't let me kill the point. Or isn't it a story for grownups?

BILL

You've heard it. About when I looked through the wrong end of a camera finder.

MARGO

(to Eve)

Remind me to tell you about when I looked into the heart of an artichoke.

EVE

I'd like to hear it.

MARGO

Some snowy night in front of the fire . . . in the meantime, while we're on the subject, will you check about the hors d'oeuvres? The caterer forgot them, the paint wasn't dry or something . . .

EVE

Of course.

She leaves. A short lull. Margo looks into cigarette boxes. Bill eyes her curiously, crosses to the fire.

BILL

Looks like I'm going to have a very fancy party . . .

MARGO

I thought you were going to be late —

BILL

When I'm guest of honor?

MARGO

I had no idea you were even here.

BILL

I ran into Eve on my way upstairs; she told me you were dressing.

MARGO

That's never stopped you before.

BILL

Well, we started talking, she wanted to know all about Hollywood, she seemed so interested . . .

MARGO

She's a girl of so many interests.

BILL

It's a pretty rare quality these days.

MARGO

She's a girl of so many rare qualities.

BILL

So she seems.

MARGO

(the steel begins to flash)

So you've pointed out, so often. So many qualities, so often. Her loyalty, efficiency, devotion, warmth, affection — and so young. So young and so fair . . .

Bill catches the drift. Incredulously.

BILL

I can't believe you're making this up — it sounds like something out of an old Clyde Fitch play . . .

MARGO

Clyde Fitch, though you may not think so, was well before my time!

BILL

(laughs)

I've always denied the legend that you were in

*Our American Cousin,* the night Lincoln was shot . . .

MARGO

I don't think that's funny!

BILL

Of course it's funny — this is all too laughable to be anything else. You know what I feel about this — this age obsession of yours — and now this ridiculous attempt to whip yourself up into a jealous froth because I spent ten minutes with a stage-struck kid —

MARGO

Twenty minutes!

BILL

Thirty minutes, forty minutes? What of it?

MARGO

Stage-struck kid . . . she's a young lady — of qualities. And I'll have you know I'm fed up with both the young lady and her qualities! Studying me as if — as if I were a play or a set of blueprints! How I walk, talk, think, eat, sleep!

BILL

Now how can you take offense at a kid trying in every way to be as much like her ideal as possible?

MARGO

Stop calling her a kid! It so happens there are particular aspects of my life to which I would like to maintain sole and exclusive rights and privileges!

BILL

For instance what?

MARGO

For instance — you!

BILL

This is my cue to take you in my arms and reassure you — but I'm not going to. I'm too mad —

MARGO

— guilty.

BILL

Mad! Darling, there are certain characteristics for which you are famous — on stage and off. I love you for some of them — and in spite of others. I haven't let those become too important to me. They're part of your equipment for getting along in what is laughingly called our environment — you've got to keep your teeth sharp. All right. But you will not sharpen them on me — or on Eve . . .

MARGO

What about her teeth? What about her fangs?

BILL

She hasn't cut them yet, and you know it! So when you start judging an idealistic dreamy-eyed *kid* by the barroom, benzedrine standards of this megalomaniac society — I won't have it! Eve Harrington has never by word, look, thought or suggestion indicated anything to me but her adoration for you and her happiness at our being in love! And to intimate anything else doesn't spell jealousy to me — it spells a paranoiac insecurity that you should be ashamed of!

MARGO

Cut! Print it! What happens in the next reel? Do I get dragged off screaming to the snake pit?

EVE'S VOICE

(quietly)

Miss Channing.

Bill and Margo look off. Eve is in the room. They have no way of knowing how long she's been there.

EVE

The hors d'oeuvres are here. Is there anything else I can do?

MARGO

Thank you, Eve. I'd like a Martini — very dry.

BILL

I'll get it.

(he crosses to Eve)

What'll you have?

Eve, involuntarily, looks to Margo.

MARGO

A milk shake?

Eve smiles, turns to Bill.

EVE

A Martini. Very dry, please.

Bill smiles back and starts across the landing toward the pantry. As he reaches the stairs, Karen, Lloyd and Max come up from the street level below. General greetings. Bill continues to the pantry. Eve and then Margo come up to add their welcome.

EVE

(to Karen)

May I have your coat?

KAREN

Don't bother, I can take it up myself . . .

EVE

Please.

Karen yields with a "Thank you, Eve." Eve goes up with the coat. Lloyd looks after her approvingly.

LLOYD

I like that girl. That quality of quiet graciousness . . .

MARGO

. . . among so many quiet qualities.

They start for the living room.

KAREN

Margo, nothing you've ever done has made me as happy as your taking Eve in . . .

MARGO

I'm so happy you're happy.

MAX

Look, you haven't been running a settlement house exactly — the kid's earned her way. You had a pretty mixed-up inventory when she took over — merchandise laying all over the shop . . .

LLOYD

You've got Margo mixed up with a five-and-ten-cent store . . .

MARGO

Make it Bergdorf Goodman . . . and now everything is on its proper shelf, eh, Max? Done up in little ribbons. I could die right now and nobody'd be confused. How about you, Max?

MAX

How about me what?

They've come to a halt near the fireplace.

MARGO

Suppose you dropped dead. What about your inventory?

MAX

I ain't gonna die. Not with a hit.

KAREN

This is the most ghoulish conversation . . .

Bill brings two Martinis. He hands one to Margo.

MARGO

(it drips ice)

Thank you.

BILL

Nothing, really.

MARGO

The kid — junior, that is — will be right down. Unless you'd like to take her drink up to her . . .

BILL

(smiles)

I can always get a fresh one. Karen — you're a Gibson girl . . .

He hands Eve's drink to Karen. Max has wandered off. Other guests are arriving. Margo gulps her drink, hands Bill the empty glass. He puts it on a passing tray. Margo takes a fresh one at the same time.

LLOYD

The general atmosphere is very Macbethish. What has or is about to happen?

MARGO

(to Bill)

What is he talking about?

BILL

Macbeth.

KAREN

(to Margo)

We know you, we've seen you before like this. Is it over — or just beginning?

Margo surveys them all.

MARGO

Fasten your seatbelts. It's going to be a bumpy night.

She downs the drink, hands the empty glass to Bill, and leaves them, CAMERA with her. She passes two women, gabbing by the piano. As they see her:

1ST WOMAN

Margo, darling!

2ND WOMAN

Darling!

MARGO

(passing)

Darlings . . .

She arrives at the landing just as Addison DeWitt comes up with MISS CASWELL. Miss Caswell is a blonde young lady, Addison's protégée-of-the-moment. Margo takes a drink from a passing tray.

MARGO

(to Addison)

I distinctly remember striking your name from the guest list. What are you doing here?

ADDISON

Dear Margo. You were an unforgettable Peter Pan — you must play it again, soon. You remember Miss Caswell?

MARGO

I do not. How do you do?

MISS CASWELL

We never met. Maybe that's why.

ADDISON

Miss Caswell is an actress. A graduate of the Copacabana School of Dramatic Arts.

(his glance is attracted by Eve coming downstairs)

Ah . . . Eve.

EVE

(deferentially)

Good evening, Mr. DeWitt.

MARGO

I had no idea you knew each other.

ADDISON

This must be, at long last, our formal introduction. Until now we have met only in passing . . .

MISS CASWELL

That's how you met me. In passing.

MARGO

(smiles)

Eve, this is an old friend of Mr. DeWitt's mother — Miss Caswell, Miss Harrington . . .

(the two girls say hello)

Addison, I've been wanting you to meet Eve for the longest time —

ADDISON

(murmurs)

It could only have been your natural timidity that kept you from mentioning it . . .

MARGO

You've heard of her great interest in the Theatre —

ADDISON

We have that in common.

MARGO

Then you two must have a long talk —

EVE

I'm afraid Mr. DeWitt would find me boring before too long.

MISS CASWELL

You won't bore him, honey. You won't even get to talk.

ADDISON

(icily)

Claudia dear, come closer.

(she does, and he points)

Do you see that little man? He is Max Fabian. He is a producer. Go do yourself some good.

MISS CASWELL

(sighs)

Why do they always look like unhappy rabbits?

ADDISON

Because that is what they are. Go make him happy.

Miss Caswell drapes her coat over the rail, heads for Max. Addison puts Eve's arm in his.

ADDISON

(to Margo)

You mustn't worry about your little charge. She is in safe hands.

MARGO

Amen.

Eve smiles uncertainly at Margo as he leads her away. Margo looks after them. She downs her drink . . .

DISSOLVE TO:

MARGO'S LIVING ROOM — NIGHT

It's many Martinis later. Most of the guests have gone. The party has reached that static state — everyone's assumed more or less permanent places.

Birdie passes, carrying a cup of coffee. CAMERA FOLLOWS her to the piano where Margo sits on the bench beside the pianist. He is just finishing "Liebestraum" and she stares moodily into a Martini. Birdie halts beside her with the coffee. Margo looks up. Birdie holds out the coffee. Margo takes the onion out of the Martini, drops it into the coffee and waves Birdie away. Birdie goes. "Liebestraum" comes to an end. The pianist tries to ease into a more sophisticated rhythm. Margo stops him.

MARGO

(quietly)
"Liebestraum."

PIANIST

I just played it.

MARGO

Play it again.

PIANIST

But that was the fourth straight time.

MARGO

Then this will be five. I suppose you think I'm too drunk to count.

PIANIST

No. You're just crazy about "Liebestraum."

MARGO

"Liebestraum."

PIANIST

Look, Miss Channing . . . it's kind of depressing. If you don't mind my saying so, everybody's kind of dying on the vine . . .

MARGO

My dear Horowitz. In the first place, I'm paying you union scale. Second, it's my piano. Third, if everybody doesn't like kind of dying on the vine, they can get off the vine and go home. "Liebestraum."

Unhappily, he plays "Liebestraum." Margo sips her Martini, stares down into it again. Bill tiptoes up.

BILL

(whispers)

Many of your guests have been wondering when they may be permitted to view the body. Where has it been laid out?

MARGO

(somberly)

It hasn't been laid out; we haven't finished with the embalming. As a matter of fact, you're looking at it. The remains of Margo Channing. Sitting up. It is my last wish to be buried sitting up.

BILL

(trying to kid her out of it)

Wouldn't you feel more natural taking a bow?

MARGO

You know nothing about feelings, natural or unnatural.

BILL

Then without feelings, your guests were also wondering whether the music couldn't be a shade more on the — shall we say, happier side.

MARGO

If my guests do not like it here, I suggest they accompany you to the nursery where I'm sure you will all feel more at home.

Bill is about to get mad — when Max bustles up.

MAX

Margo. You by any chance got bicarbonate of soda in the house?

MARGO

(sympathetic)

Poor Max. Heartburn?

(Max nods)

It's that Miss Caswell. I don't know why she doesn't give Addison heartburn.

BILL

No heart to burn.

MARGO

Everybody has a heart — except some people.

(she finishes her drink, stands up)

Of course I've got bicarb. There's a box in the

pantry. We'll put your name on it. Max Fabian. It'll stay there. Always. Just for you.

MAX

(touched)

Let the rest of the world beat their brains out for a buck. It's friends that count. And I got friends.

MARGO

I love you, Max. I really mean it. I love you. Come to the pantry.

She takes off. Max waits to set Bill straight.

MAX

She loves me like a father. Also, she's loaded.

He starts after Margo. As the CAMERA PANS with Bill we see Margo going into the pantry with Max following her. Bill joins Addison and Miss Caswell on the stairs.

PANTRY — NIGHT

It's a good-sized one. Margo crosses to a cupboard. She finds the bicarb.

MARGO

Here you are, Maxie dear. One good burp and you'll be rid of that Miss Caswell . . .

MAX

The situation I'm in ain't the kind you can belch your way out of. I made a promise . . .

MARGO

To Miss Caswell?

(Max nods)

What?

MAX

An audition for the part we're replacing. What's-her-name, your sister . . .

He adds water to the bicarb.

MARGO

Well, if she can act, she might not be bad. She looks like she might burn down a plantation . . .

MAX

(mixing)

I feel right now like there's one burning in me.

MARGO

When's the audition?

MAX

A couple of weeks.

MARGO

I tell you what. Why don't I read with her?

MAX

Would you?

MARGO

Anything to help you out, Max.

MAX

(drinking)

This is real co-operation. I appreciate it.

MARGO

Not at all. And you could do me a big favor, if you would —

MAX

All you got to do is name it.

MARGO

Give Eve Harrington a job in your office.

Max burps.

MARGO

You get quick action, don't you?

MAX

Margo, I wouldn't think of taking that girl away from you . . .

MARGO

You said yourself my inventory is in good shape — all of my merchandise put away. To keep her here with nothing to do — I'd be standing in her way . . . and you need her, Max.

MAX

But what could she do?

MARGO

She'd be a great help — read scripts, interview people you have to see, get rid of the ones you don't have to . . . you'd be a man of leisure —

MAX

Well . . .

MARGO

Think of your health, Max — more time to relax, play some cards.

MAX

I don't know if this would be a wise move . . .

MARGO

Promise.

MAX

I promise.

MARGO

(happily)

That's my Max.

Lloyd enters, looking for her.

LLOYD

There you are, both of you. Max, Karen has decided it's time to go . . .

MARGO

Where is she?

LLOYD

Up in your room.

MAX

If you'll excuse me —

(to Margo)

I'll go tell Miss Caswell . . .

MARGO

Watch out for heartburn.

MAX

I ain't worried so much now. It's nearly time for my powder.

He goes out. A pause.

MARGO

Who's left out there?

LLOYD

Too many. And you've got a new guest. A movie star from Hollywood.

MARGO

Shucks. And my autograph book is at the cleaners.

Another pause.

MARGO

You disapprove of me when I'm like this, don't you?

LLOYD

Not exactly. Sometimes, though, I wish I understood you better.

MARGO

When you do, let me in on it.

LLOYD

I will.

Another pause.

MARGO

How's the new one coming?

LLOYD

The play? All right, I guess . . .

MARGO

"Cora." She's — still a girl of twenty?

LLOYD

Twentyish. It isn't important.

MARGO

Don't you think it's about time it became important?

LLOYD

How do you mean?

MARGO

Don't be evasive.

LLOYD

Margo, you haven't got any age.

MARGO

Miss Channing is ageless. Spoken like a press agent.

LLOYD

I know what I'm talking about. After all, they're my plays . . .

MARGO

Spoken like an author.

(abruptly)

Lloyd, I'm not twentyish. I am not thirtyish. Three months ago, I was forty years old. Forty. Four oh.

(she smiles)

That slipped out, I hadn't quite made up my mind to admit it. Now I feel as if I'd suddenly taken all my clothes off . . .

LLOYD

Week after week, to thousands of people, you're as young as you want . . .

MARGO

. . . as young as they want, you mean. And I'm not interested in whether thousands of people think I'm six or six hundred —

LLOYD

Just one person. Isn't that so?

(Margo doesn't answer)

You know what this is all about, don't you? It has very little to do with whether you should play "Cora" — it has everything to do with the fact you've had another fight with Bill.

A pause. Margo closes the box of bicarb.

MARGO

Bill's thirty-two. He looks thirty-two. He looked it five years ago, he'll look it twenty years from now. I hate men.

(she puts the box down)

Don't worry, Lloyd. I'll play your play. I'll wear rompers and come in rolling a hoop if you like . . .

MARGO'S BEDROOM — NIGHT

The bed is littered with fur coats. Karen is making repairs at Margo's dressing table. Eve enters, carrying a magnificent sable coat which she drops on the bed.

KAREN

Now who'd show up at this hour? It's time people went home — hold that coat up . . .

(Eve holds it up. Karen whistles)

. . . whose is it?

EVE

Some Hollywood movie star. Her plane got in late.

KAREN

Discouraging, isn't it? Women with furs like that where it never even gets cold . . .

EVE

Hollywood.

KAREN

Tell me, Eve — how are things going with you? Happy?

Eve melts into warmth. She beams, sits on the bed. Karen has spun around on the dressing-table stool.

EVE

There should be a new word for happiness. Being here with Miss Channing has been — I just can't say, she's been so wonderful, done so much for me —

KAREN

(smiles)

Lloyd says Margo compensates for underplaying on the stage by overplaying reality . . .

(she gets up, gets her own coat)

. . . next to that sable, my new mink seems like an old bedjacket . . . you've done your share, Eve. You've worked wonders with Margo . . .

She starts out.

EVE

(hesitantly)

Mrs. Richards . . .

KAREN

(pauses, smiles)

Karen.

EVE

Karen . . .

(she picks at the coverlet)

. . . isn't it awful, I'm about to ask you for another favor — after all you've done already.

KAREN

(crosses to her)

Nobody's done so much, Eve. You've got to stop thinking of yourself as one of the Hundred Neediest Cases . . . what is it?

EVE

Well . . . Miss Channing's affairs are in such good shape . . . there isn't enough to keep me as busy as I should be, really — not that I'd even consider anything that would take me away from her . . . but the other day — when I heard Mr. Fabian tell Miss Channing that her understudy was going to have a baby, and they'd have to replace her . . .

She looks down at the coverlet once more.

KAREN

You want to be Margo's new understudy . . .

EVE

I don't let myself think about it, even —

(she looks up, rises as she speaks)

— but I do know the part so well, and every bit of the staging, there'd be no need to break in a new girl —

(suddenly afraid, she sits)

— but suppose I had to go on one night? To an audience that came to see Margo Channing. No, I couldn't possibly . . .

KAREN

(laughs)

Don't worry too much about that. Margo just doesn't miss performances. If she can walk, crawl or roll — she plays.

EVE

(nods proudly)

The show must go on.

KAREN

No, dear. Margo must go on.

(she sits beside Eve)

As a matter of fact, I see no reason why you shouldn't be Margo's understudy . . .

EVE

Do you think Miss Channing would approve?

KAREN

I think she'd cheer.

EVE

But Mr. Richards and Mr. Sampson —

KAREN

They'll do as they're told.

Eve smiles a little. A pause.

EVE

Then — would you talk to Mr. Fabian about it?

KAREN

Of course.

EVE

You won't forget it?

KAREN

I won't forget.

EVE

I seem to be forever thanking you for something, don't I?

She hugs Karen, leaves. She nearly collides with Birdie on her way in.

BIRDIE

The bed looks like a dead animal act. Which one is sables?

KAREN

(pointing)

But she just got here . . .

BIRDIE

She's on her way. With half the men in the joint.

(she holds up the coat)

It's only a fur coat . . .

KAREN

What did you expect — live sables?

BIRDIE

A diamond collar, gold sleeves — you know, picture people . . .

They start out.

KAREN

Bill says actors out there eat just as infrequently as here —

BIRDIE

They can always grab oranges off trees. This you can't do in Times Square . . .

Through the open door, we see them go down the stairs and out of sight.

SECOND FLOOR LANDING AND STAIRS

CAMERA PULLS BACK with Karen and Birdie as they come down into the scene, until IT discloses Bill, Max, Addison, Miss Caswell — and, at the feet of Bill and Addison . . . Eve. They are all seated on the steps.

Birdie goes through and down the stairs to the first floor. Karen remains with the others.

Addison is holding forth:

ADDISON

Every now and then, some elder statesman of the theatre or cinema assures the public that actors and actresses are just plain folks. Ignoring the fact that their greatest attraction to the public is their complete lack of resemblance to normal human beings . . .

MISS CASWELL

(as Birdie and the sables pass)

Now there's something a girl could make sacrifices for.

BILL

And probably has.

MISS CASWELL

Sable.

MAX

(to Miss Caswell)

Did you say sable — or Gable?

MISS CASWELL

Either one.

ADDISON

It is senseless to insist that theatrical folk are no different from the good people of Des Moines, Chillicothe or Liverpool. By and large we are concentrated gatherings of neurotics, egomaniacs, emotional misfits, and precocious children —

MAX

(to Bill)

Gable. Why a feller like that don't come East to do a play . . .

BILL

(nods)

He must be miserable, the life he lives out there —

ADDISON

These so-called abnormalities — they're our stock in trade, they make us actors, writers, directors, et cetera, in the first place —

MAX

Answer me this. What makes a man become a producer?

ADDISON

What makes a man walk into a lion cage with nothing but a chair?

MAX

This answer satisfies me a hundred per cent.

ADDISON

We all have abnormality in common. We are a breed apart from the rest of humanity, we theatre folk. We are the original displaced personalities . . .

BILL

(laughs; to Eve)

You won't have to read his column tomorrow — you just heard it. I don't agree, Addison . . .

ADDISON

That happens to be your particular abnormality.

BILL

Oh, I'll admit there's a screwball element in the theatre. It sticks out, it's got spotlights on it and a brass band. But it isn't basic, it isn't standard — if it were, the theatre couldn't survive . . .

MISS CASWELL

(to a passing butler)

Oh, waiter . . .

The butler goes right by.

ADDISON

That isn't a waiter, my dear. That's a butler.

MISS CASWELL

Well, I can't yell "Oh, butler," can I? Maybe somebody's name is Butler . . .

ADDISON

You have a point. An idiotic one, but a point.

MISS CASWELL

I don't want to make trouble. All I want is a drink.

MAX

(getting up)

Leave me get you one . . .

MISS CASWELL

(pitching)

Oh, thank you, Mr. Fabian.

Max leaves with her empty glass.

ADDISON

Well done. I see your career rising in the East like the sun . . .

(to Bill)

. . . you were saying?

BILL

I was saying that the theatre is nine-tenths hard work. Work done the hard way — by sweat, application and craftsmanship. I'll agree to this — that to be a good actor, actress, or anything else in the theatre, means wanting to be that more than anything else in the world . . .

EVE

(abruptly)

Yes. Yes, it does . . .

BILL

(goes on)

It means a concentration of ambition, desire and sacrifice such as no other profession demands . . . and I'll agree that the man or woman who accepts those terms can't be ordinary, can't be — just someone. To give so much for almost always so little . . .

Eve speaks almost as if unaware of what she says. She looks at no one in particular, just off . . .

EVE

So little. So little, did you say? Why, if there's nothing else — there's applause. I've listened, from backstage, to people applaud. It's like — like waves of love coming over the footlights and wrapping you up. Imagine . . . to know, every night, that different hundreds of people love you . . . they smile, their eyes shine — you've pleased them, they want you, you belong. Just that alone is worth anything . . .

She becomes aware of Addison's strange smile, of Bill's look of warm interest. She's embarrassed, she turns away — then scrambles to her feet as Margo approaches with Lloyd from the direction of the pantry.

Margo's fake smile fades as Eve gets up. She's unpleasant and depressed.

MARGO

Don't get up. And please stop acting as if I were the queen mother.

EVE

(hurt)

I'm sorry, I didn't mean to —

BILL

(sharply)

Outside of a beehive, Margo, your behavior would hardly be considered either queenly or motherly!

MARGO

You're *in* a beehive, pal, didn't you know? We're all busy little bees, full of stings, making honey day and night —

(to Eve)

— aren't we, honey?

KAREN

Margo, really . . .

MARGO

Please don't play governess, Karen. I haven't your unyielding good taste; I wish I'd gone to Radcliffe too but Father wouldn't hear of it — he needed help at the notions counter . . .

(to Addison)

I'm being rude now, aren't I? Or should I say "ain't I"?

ADDISON

You're maudlin and full of self-pity. You're magnificent.

Max has come up with Miss Caswell's drink.

LLOYD

How about calling it a night?

MARGO

And you pose as a playwright. A situation pregnant with possibilities — and all you can think of is everybody go to sleep . . .

BILL

It's a good thought.

MARGO

It won't play.

KAREN

As a nonprofessional, I think it's an excellent idea. Undramatic, but practical . . .

As she speaks, she makes her way to Lloyd's side.

MARGO

Happy little housewife . . .

BILL

Cut it out.

MARGO

This is my house, not a theatre! In my house you're a guest, not a director —

KAREN

Then stop being a star — stop treating your guests as your supporting cast!

ADDISON

Hear, hear . . .

LLOYD

Now let's not get into a big hassel —

KAREN

It's about time we did! It's about time Margo realized that what's attractive on stage need not necessarily be attractive off!

MARGO

(suddenly)

All right! I'm going to bed.

(to Bill)

You be the host. It's your party. Happy birthday, welcome home, and we-who-are-about-to-die-salute-you . . .

She starts upstairs.

BILL

Need any help?

MARGO

(pauses, smiles)

To put me to bed? Take my clothes off, hold my head, tuck me in, turn out the lights, tiptoe out . . . ? Eve would. Wouldn't you, Eve?

EVE

If you'd like.

MARGO

I wouldn't like.

She goes out, exits out of sight. A pause. Miss Caswell reaches up to take the drink out of Max's hand.

MAX

I forgot I had it.

MISS CASWELL

I didn't.

Bill gets up and goes after Margo.

ADDISON

Too bad. We'll miss the third act. They're going to play it off stage.

Eve turns away abruptly, in sudden tears.

LLOYD

Coming?

KAREN

In a minute . . .

She crosses to Eve, puts an arm around her.

KAREN

You mustn't mind Margo too much, even if I do . . .

EVE

But there must be some reason, something I've done without knowing . . .

KAREN

The reason is Margo and don't try to figure it out. Einstein couldn't.

EVE

If I thought I'd offended her, of all people —

KAREN

Eve. I'm fond of Margo, too. But I know Margo.

And every now and then there is nothing I want to do so much as to kick her right square in the pants.

EVE

(smiles)

Well — if she's got to pick on someone, I'd just as soon it was me.

Karen smiles back. She joins Lloyd and Max.

LLOYD

Max is going to drop us.

ADDISON

I've often wondered, Max, why you bother with a chauffeur and limousine in New York City.

MAX

In my case it's necessary. Too many taxi drivers write plays.

ADDISON

And too many of them are produced.

MISS CASWELL

Let's go sit by the piano.

ADDISON

You have me confused with Dan Dailey. You go sit by the piano.

(to Eve)

And you come sit by me.

(to the others)

Good night.

They laugh, say "good night," and start downstairs. As Eve crosses to Addison:

EVE

Karen . . .

(Karen pauses)

. . . you won't forget will you? What we talked about before?

KAREN

(smiles)

No, Eve. I won't forget.

She follows the men downstairs. CAMERA MOVES to a CLOSEUP of an old engraving of Mrs. Siddons as "The Tragic Muse" which hangs among other theatrical mementos on the stair wall . . .

FADE OUT

FADE IN

NEW YORK THEATRE — DAY

Margo gets out of a cab in front of the theatre and goes in. It's a Friday afternoon — no performance.

LOBBY AND FOYER — DAY

Margo comes from the street through the lobby (a few people buying tickets) and into the deserted foyer. She spots Addison sprawled on one of the sofas.

MARGO

Why so remote, Addison? I should think you'd be at the side of your protégée, lending her moral support.

ADDISON

Miss Caswell, at the moment, is where I can lend no support — moral or otherwise.

MARGO

The ladies' — shall we say — lounge?

ADDISON

Being violently ill to her tummy.

MARGO

It's good luck before an audition. She'll be all right once it starts.

She heads for the auditorium.

ADDISON

Miss Caswell got lucky too late. The audition is over.

MARGO

(stops)

Over? It can't be. I've come to read with her. I promised Max.

ADDISON

The audition was called for 2:30. It is now nearly four.

MARGO

(lightly)

Is it really? I must start wearing a watch, I never do, you know . . . who read with Miss Caswell? Bill?

(he shakes his head)

Lloyd?

(he shakes his head)

Well, it couldn't have been Max! Who?

ADDISON

Naturally enough, your understudy.

MARGO

I consider it highly unnatural to allow a girl in an advanced state of pregnancy —

ADDISON

I refer to your new and unpregnant understudy. Eve Harrington.

MARGO

Eve! My understudy . . .

ADDISON

(keenly)

Didn't you know?

MARGO

(quickly)

Of course I knew.

ADDISON

It just slipped your mind.

A moment of silence.

MARGO

How . . . how was Miss Caswell?

ADDISON

Frankly, I don't remember.

MARGO

Just slipped your mind.

ADDISON

Completely. Nor, I am sure, could anyone else present tell you how Miss Caswell read, or whether Miss Caswell read or rode a pogo stick . . .

MARGO

Was she that bad?

As Addison speaks, he rises with excitement.

ADDISON

Margo, as you know, I have lived in the Theatre as a Trappist monk lives in his faith. I have no other world, no other life — and once in a great while I experience that moment of Revelation for which all true believers wait and pray. You were one. Jeanne Eagels another . . . Paula Wessely . . . Hayes — there are others, three or four. Eve Harrington will be among them . . .

MARGO

(flatly)

I take it she read well.

ADDISON

It wasn't a reading, it was a performance. Brilliant, vivid, something made of music and fire . . .

MARGO

How nice.

ADDISON

In time she'll be what you are.

MARGO

A mass of music and fire. That's me. An old kazoo and some sparklers. Tell me — was Bill swept away, too, or were you too full of Revelation to notice?

ADDISON

Bill didn't say — but Lloyd was beside himself. He listened to his play as if someone else had written it, he said. It sounded so fresh, so new, so full of meaning . . .

MARGO

How nice for Lloyd. And how nice for Eve. How nice for everybody.

Addison, of course, knows exactly what he's doing. He senses the approaching typhoon, he whips it up.

ADDISON

Eve was incredibly modest. She insisted that no credit was due her, that Lloyd felt as he did only because she read his lines exactly as he had written them.

MARGO

The implication being that I have not been reading them as written?

ADDISON

To the best of my recollection, neither your name nor your performance entered the conversation.

Miss Caswell appears, uncertainly, in the background.

ADDISON

Feeling better, my dear?

MISS CASWELL

Like I just swam the English Channel. Now what?

ADDISON

Your next move, it seems to me, should be toward television.

Margo, abruptly, starts for the auditorium. Addison smiles. He takes Miss Caswell's arm.

MISS CASWELL

Tell me this. Do they have auditions for television?

ADDISON

That's all television is, my dear. Nothing but auditions.

He leads her toward the street.

THEATRE

The curtain is up; the set, covered, is a bedroom in a deteriorating Southern mansion.

There is no one in the theatre but Max, seated on the aisle about two-thirds down, and Eve with Lloyd and Bill on the stage. She is seated; they stand between her and the auditorium. There is some ad-lib talk among the three which we cannot make out. CAMERA is on Margo marching down the aisle with a steady pace.

She passes Max who smiles a sickly, hopeful smile. She ignores him as if he were a used paper cup. She disappears through the door which leads backstage.

Max whistles. Lloyd turns. Max indicates the door and puts his hands to his head in despair.

Margo walks out of the wings on stage. Bill and Lloyd turn to her. Eve rises.

MARGO

(cheerily)

Terribly sorry I'm late, lunch was long and I couldn't find a cab — where's Miss Caswell, shall we start? Oh, hello, Eve . . .

EVE

Hello, Miss Channing.

MARGO

How are you making out in Mr. Fabian's office?

(over the footlights to Max)

I don't want you working the child too hard, Max — just because you promised. As you see, I kept my promise, too . . .

Max slumps in his seat. By the time Margo turns back to them, the others have exchanged swift looks.

BILL

It's all over.

MARGO

What's all over?

BILL

The audition. Eve read with Miss Caswell.

MARGO

(pleased astonishment)

Eve?

(she turns to her)

How enchanting.

(to Lloyd and Bill)

Wherever did you two get the idea of having Eve read with Miss Caswell?

LLOYD

She's your understudy.

MARGO

Eve? Eve, my understudy? But I had no idea . . .

LLOYD

I thought you knew. She was put on over a week ago —

MARGO

It seems almost inconceivable that I haven't seen her backstage, but with so many people loitering about . . . well, well. So Eve is not working for Max after all —

(out to Max again)

— Max, you sly puss.

Max submerges further in his seat.

EVE

Miss Channing, I can't tell you how glad I am that you arrived so late.

MARGO

Really, Eve? Why?

EVE

Well, if you'd been here to begin with, I wouldn't have dared to read at all . . .

MARGO

Why not?

EVE

. . . and if you'd come in the middle, I'd have stopped, I couldn't have gone on —

MARGO

(murmurs)

What a pity, all that fire and music being turned off . . .

BILL

What fire and music?

MARGO

You wouldn't understand.

(to Lloyd)

How was Miss Caswell?

LLOYD

Back to the Copacabana. But Eve. Margo, let me tell you about Eve —

EVE

(breaking in)

I was dreadful, Miss Channing, believe me — I have no right to be anyone's understudy, much less yours . . .

MARGO

I'm sure you underestimate yourself, Eve. You always do.

(to Lloyd)

You were about to tell me about Eve . . .

LLOYD

You'd have been proud of her.

MARGO

I'm sure . . .

LLOYD

She was a revelation . . .

MARGO

To you, too?

LLOYD

What do you mean?

MARGO

(the ice begins to form)

I mean, among other things, that it must have been a revelation to have your twenty-four-year-old character played by a twenty-four-year-old actress.

LLOYD

That's beside the point.

MARGO

It's right to the point. Also that it must have sounded so new and fresh to you — so exciting to have the lines read just as you wrote them!

BILL

Addison — !

MARGO

So full of meaning, fire and music!

LLOYD

You've been talking to that venomous fishwife, Addison DeWitt —

MARGO

— in this case, apparently, as trustworthy as the World Almanac!

LLOYD

You knew when you came in that the audition was over, that Eve was your understudy! Playing that childish little game of cat-and-mouse . . .

MARGO

Not mouse, never mouse! If anything — rat!

LLOYD

You have a genius for making a barroom brawl out of a perfectly innocent misunderstanding at most!

MARGO

Perfectly innocent! Men have been hanged for less! I'm lied to, attacked behind my back, accused of reading your silly dialogue inaccurately — as if it were Holy Gospel!

LLOYD

I never said it was!

MARGO

When you listened as if someone else had written your play — whom did you have in mind? Sherwood? Arthur Miller? Beaumont and Fletcher?

Max has edged his way to the stage.

MAX

(from below)

May I say a word?

LLOYD

No!

(to Margo)

What makes you think that either Miller or

Sherwood would stand for the nonsense I take from you — you'd better stick to Beaumont and Fletcher! They've been dead for three hundred years!

He stalks into the wings. Bill's reaction to the fight is typical. He lights a cigarette, stretches out on the covered bed. Eve stands frozen with fear. Margo yells after Lloyd into the wings.

MARGO

And they're getting better performances today than they ever got! *All* playwrights should be dead for three hundred years!

Lloyd comes out of the door leading to the auditorium. The battle goes on without a pause. As he yells back, he crosses to Max at row A, center.

LLOYD

That would solve none of their problems — because actresses never die! The stars never die and never change!

He starts up the aisle with Max.

MARGO

You can change this star any time you want! For a new, fresh, exciting one fully equipped with fire and music! Any time you want — starting with tonight's performance!

Now it's Max who stops and shouts back at her.

MAX

This is for lawyers to talk about, this concerns a run-of-the-play contract, and this you can't rewrite or ad lib!

MARGO

(from the stage)

Are you threatening me with legal action, Mr. Fabian?

MAX

Are you breaking the contract?

MARGO

Answer my question!

MAX

Who am I to threaten? I'm a dying man.

MARGO

I didn't hear you!

MAX

(yelling)

I said I'm a dying man!

MARGO

Not until the last drugstore has sold its last pill!

LLOYD

(from the top of the aisle)

I shall never understand the weird process by

which a body with a voice suddenly fancies itself as a mind! Just when exactly does an actress decide they're *her* words she's saying and *her* thoughts she's expressing?

MARGO

Usually at the point when she's got to rewrite and re-think them to keep the audience from leaving the theatre!

LLOYD

It's about time the piano realized it has not written the concerto!

Max has already walked out unhappily. Lloyd now slams out. Margo glares after him, then turns to Bill who smokes his cigarette peacefully on the bed.

MARGO

(quiet menace)

And you, I take it, are the Paderewski who plays his concerto on me, the piano?

(Bill waves his cigarette; he's noncommittal)

Where is Princess Fire-and-Music?

BILL

Who?

MARGO

The kid. Junior.

BILL

(looks lazily)

Gone.

MARGO

I must have frightened her away.

BILL

I wouldn't be surprised. Sometimes you frighten me.

MARGO

(paces up and down)

Poor little flower. Just dropped her petals and folded her tent . . .

BILL

Don't mix your metaphors.

MARGO

I'll mix what I like.

BILL

Okay. Mix.

MARGO

I'm nothing but a body with a voice. No mind.

BILL

What a body, what a voice.

MARGO

That ex-ship news reporter. No body, no voice, *all* mind!

BILL

The gong rang. The fight's over. Calm down.

MARGO

I will not calm down!

BILL

Don't calm down.

MARGO

You're being terribly tolerant, aren't you?

BILL

I'm trying terribly hard.

MARGO

Well, you needn't. I will not be tolerated. And I will not be plotted against!

BILL

Here we go . . .

MARGO

Such nonsense, what do you all take me for — little Nell from the country? Been my understudy for over a week without my knowing, carefully hidden no doubt —

BILL

(sits up)

Now don't get carried away —

MARGO

(going right on)

— shows up for an audition when everyone knew

I'd be here . . . and gives a performance! Out of nowhere — gives a performance!

BILL

You've been all through that with Lloyd —

MARGO

The playwright doesn't make the performance — and it doesn't just happen! And this one didn't — full of fire and music and what-not, it was carefully rehearsed I have no doubt, over and over, full of those Bill Sampson touches!

BILL

I am sick and tired of these paranoiac outbursts!

MARGO

Paranoiac!

BILL

I didn't know Eve Harrington was your understudy until half past two this afternoon!

MARGO

Tell that to Dr. Freud! Along with the rest of it . . .

She turns away. Bill grabs her, pulls her down on the bed. He holds her down.

BILL

No, I'll tell it to you! For the last time, I'll tell it to you. Because you've got to stop hurting yourself, and me, and the two of us by these paranoiac tantrums!

MARGO

(struggling)

That word again! I don't even know what it means . . .

BILL

(firmly)

It's about time you found out. I love you.

(Margo says "Ha!")

I love you. You're a beautiful and intelligent woman —

(Margo says "A body with a voice")

— a beautiful and intelligent woman and a great actress —

(he waits. Margo says nothing)

— at the peak of her career. You have every reason for happiness —

(Margo says "Except happiness")

— every reason, but due to some strange, uncontrollable, unconscious drive you permit the slightest action of a kid —

(Margo sneers "Kid!")

— kid like Eve to turn you into an hysterical, screaming harpy! Now once and for all, stop it!

Margo seems quiet. He gets up. She sits up.

MARGO

It's obvious you're not a woman.

BILL

I've been aware of that for some time.

MARGO

Well, I am.

BILL

I'll say.

MARGO

Don't be condescending.

BILL

Come on, get up. I'll buy you a drink.

MARGO

(with dignity)

I admit I may have seen better days, but I am still not to be had for the price of a cocktail — like a salted peanut.

BILL

(laughs)

Margo, let's make peace.

MARGO

The terms are too high. Unconditional surrender.

BILL

Just being happy? Just stopping all this nonsense about Eve — and Eve and me?

MARGO

It's not nonsense.

BILL

But if I tell you it is — as I just did. Were you listening to me?

(Margo nods)

Isn't that enough?

MARGO

I wish it were.

BILL

Then what would be enough?

(Margo doesn't answer)

If we got married?

MARGO

I wouldn't want you to marry me just to prove something.

BILL

You've had so many reasons for not wanting to marry me . . . Margo, tell me what's behind all this.

MARGO

I — I don't know, Bill. Just a feeling, I don't know . . .

BILL

I think you do know but you won't or can't tell me.

(Margo doesn't say)

I said before it was going to be my last try, and I meant it. I can't think of anything else to do. I wish I could.

(a pause)

We usually wind up screaming and throwing things as the curtain comes down. Then it comes up again and everything's fine. But not this time.

(he takes a breath)

You know there isn't a playwright in the world who could make me believe this would happen between two adult people. Good-bye, Margo.

No word from her. He starts away.

MARGO

Bill . . .

(he stops)

. . . where are you going? To find Eve?

BILL

(smiles grimly)

That suddenly makes the whole thing believable.

He goes out. Margo, alone, sits for a moment sadly. Then she begins to cry . . .

FADE OUT

FADE IN

RICHARDS' STUDIO APARTMENT — DAY

One large room, a small foyer with a door to the corridor. A stair up one wall to a narrow balcony from which a couple of bedrooms open.

Karen is painting. Earnestly but badly. A still life of an orange, an avocado, an eggplant and three bananas.

KAREN'S VOICE

*On the day of the audition, my biggest worry was to keep a banana from looking like part of an eggplant . . . then Lloyd came home.*

(in the background, Lloyd lets himself in)

*It was right after his brawl with Margo . . .*

Lloyd slams the door, flings his hat away, strides in, peeling off muffler and overcoat.

KAREN

Lloyd, what's happened?

LLOYD

Up to here! That's where I've got it — up to here! Of all the star-ridden, presumptuous, hysterical —

KAREN

Margo, again . . .

LLOYD

And again and again! Two hours late for the audition, to begin with —

KAREN

That's on time for Margo.

LLOYD

Then a childish, heavy-handed routine about not knowing Eve was her understudy —

KAREN

It's just possible she didn't . . .

LLOYD

Of course she knew! For one thing, Addison told her how superbly Eve had read the part — !

(suddenly softening)

Karen, let me tell you about Eve. She's got everything — a born actress. Sensitive, understanding, young, exciting, vibrant —

KAREN

— don't run out of adjectives, dear.

LLOYD

— everything a playwright first thinks of wanting to write about . . . until his play becomes a vehicle for Miss Channing.

KAREN

Margo hasn't done badly by it.

LLOYD

Margo. Margo's great. She knows it. That's the trouble. She can play Peck's Bad Boy all she wants, and who's to stop her? Who's to give her that boot in the rear she needs and deserves?

He starts up the stairs to a bedroom.

KAREN

(murmurs)

It's going to be a cozy week-end.

LLOYD

(pauses)

What is?

KAREN

We're driving out to the country tomorrow night. Just the four of us. Bill, Margo, you and I . . .

LLOYD

Well. We've spent week-ends before with nobody talking . . .

(continues up the stairs)

. . . just be sure to lock up all blunt instruments and throwable objects.

As he goes into one of the bedrooms, Karen sits thoughtfully on a couch. She muses . . .

KAREN'S VOICE

*Newton—they say, thought of gravity by getting*

*hit on the head by an apple. And the man who invented the steam engine, he was watching a tea-kettle . . . but not me. My Big Idea came to me just sitting on a couch . . .*

She lies down, folds her hands behind her head.

KAREN'S VOICE

*That boot in the rear to Margo. Heaven knows she had one coming. From me, from Lloyd, from Eve, Bill, Max, and so on — we'd all felt those size fives of hers often enough . . . but how? The answer was buzzing around me like a fly . . .*

She sits up. She smiles. The smile fades . . .

KAREN'S VOICE

*I had it. But I let it go. Screaming and calling names is one thing — but this could mean . . .*

She shakes her head, crosses to her easel, resumes work on the bananas. She slows down, then stops.

KAREN'S VOICE

*Why not? Why, I said to myself, not? It would all seem perfectly legitimate. And there were only two people in the world who would know. Also, the boot would land where it would do the most good for all concerned —*

She puts the brush away and crosses to the phone which is by Lloyd's work chair. As she crosses:

KAREN'S VOICE

*And after all, it was no more than a perfectly harmless joke which Margo, herself, would be the first to enjoy . . .*

She looks in a leather phone book, picks up the phone and dials.

KAREN'S VOICE

*. . . and no reason why she shouldn't be told about it — in time.*

There's an answer at the other end.

KAREN

(into phone)

Hello . . . will you call Miss Eve Harrington to the phone, please? Not at all . . . thank you.

And as she waits, we

DISSOLVE TO:

COUNTRYSIDE — NIGHT

Open country. Preferably no houses in sight. Plenty of snow. Lloyd's car drives along.

KAREN'S VOICE

*It was a cold week-end — outside and in. Bill didn't come at all. Margo didn't know where he was and didn't care — she kept saying. Somehow we staggered through Sunday — and by the time we drove Margo to the station late Monday afternoon, she and Lloyd had thawed out to the extent of being civil to each other . . .*

INSIDE LLOYD'S COUPE — NIGHT

Lloyd driving. All three in the front seat.

KAREN

What time is it?

LLOYD

When you asked a minute ago it was five-forty-two. It is now five-forty-three. When you ask again a minute from now, it will be —

KAREN

I just don't want Margo to miss her train. As it is, she'll barely make the theatre . . .

LLOYD

Five-fifty-five. We'll be at the station in plenty of time.

MARGO

That little place just two hours from New York. It's on my list of things-I'll-never-understand. Like collecting shrunken Indian heads . . .

KAREN

Of all people you should know what it means to want some peace and quiet —

MARGO

Peace and quiet is for libraries.

The car swerves — suddenly and slightly.

KAREN

Lloyd, be careful . . .

LLOYD

Just a little skid, that's all. This road's like glass.

MARGO

Karen and I just don't want an accident —

LLOYD

I have no intention of having an accident!

MARGO

It's not important whether you do. We are wearing long underwear.

They all laugh. Suddenly the car slows and stops — with that hissing sound that can mean only one thing — no gas.

LLOYD

Now what's this . . . ?

He tries to start it again. No luck. He turns on the dashboard lights. The gas gauge reads empty.

LLOYD

But it can't be! We can't be out of gas! I filled it myself yesterday!

(to Karen)

Wasn't it full when you drove to Brewster this morning?

KAREN

(very low)

I guess I didn't look. You know I don't pay attention to those things . . .

LLOYD

Incredible . . .

Futilely, he runs the starter again.

MARGO

(crisply)

How much time have we?

LLOYD

Roughly ten minutes.

MARGO

How far to the station?

LLOYD

Three or four miles . . .

MARGO

Any houses or farms around where we can borrow gas?

LLOYD

(looking)

None in sight, there aren't many along this back road . . .

MARGO

Not many cars either, not much chance of a lift . . .

A moment of silence.

LLOYD

Well. No sense my just sitting here. I'm going to walk up about half a mile, just in case.

He starts out of the car. The cold comes in like a knife, the women react.

KAREN

You'll break your neck on that ice.

LLOYD

(grins)

What a way to die — trying to get an actress to the theatre in time. Tell Max I want to be buried with my royalties . . .

KAREN

Don't joke about such things.

MARGO

(quietly)

How fortunate that I have an understudy so ready, so willing and so able to go on.

LLOYD

The audience will want its money refunded, believe me.

MARGO

Thank you, Lloyd. Godspeed.

Lloyd starts down the road. He slips once, recovers, waves and keeps going.

KAREN

He always looks so pathetic whenever he does anything physical —

MARGO

It seems to me that walking, for most people, is not very dangerous.

KAREN

(smiles)

I just never think of Lloyd as anywhere but indoors and anything but sitting down.

MARGO

Be brave. He'll come back — with or without gas.

They tuck the fur car robe about them. A pause. Margo turns on the radio . . . it's "Liebestraum."

MARGO

Do you want it on?

KAREN

It doesn't matter.

MARGO

I detest cheap sentiment.

She turns it off. Another pause.

MARGO

Karen.

(Karen says "hm?")

I haven't been very pleasant this week-end.

KAREN

We've all seemed a little tense lately . . .

MARGO

Come to think of it, I haven't been very pleasant for weeks. For that, I'm truly sorry. More than any two people I know, I don't want you and Lloyd to be angry with me . . .

KAREN

We're never deeply angry, we just get sore. The way you do. We know you too well . . .

MARGO

So many people — know me. I wish I did. I wish someone would tell me about me . . .

KAREN

You're Margo. Just — Margo.

MARGO

And what is that? Besides something spelled out in light bulbs, I mean. Besides something called a temperament, which consists mostly of swooping about on a broomstick screaming at the top of my voice . . . infants behave the way I do, you know. They carry on and misbehave — they'd get drunk if they knew how — when they can't have what they want. When they feel unwanted or insecure — or unloved . . .

There's a pause.

KAREN

What about Bill?

MARGO

What about Bill?

KAREN

He's in love with you.

MARGO

More than anything in this world, I love Bill. And I want Bill. I want him to want me. But me. Not Margo Channing. And if I can't tell them apart — how can he?

KAREN

Why should he — and why should you?

MARGO

Bill's in love with Margo Channing. He's fought with her, worked with her, loved her . . . but ten years from now — Margo Channing will have ceased to exist. And what's left will be . . . what?

KAREN

Margo. Bill is all of eight years younger than you.

MARGO

Those years stretch as the years go on. I've seen it happen too often.

KAREN

Not to you. Not to Bill.

MARGO

Isn't that what they always say?

She turns the radio on again. A piano nocturne . . .

MARGO

I don't suppose the heater runs when the motor doesn't?

KAREN

Silly, isn't it? You'd think they'd fix it so people could just sit in a car and keep warm . . .

Margo nods, gets some cigarettes out of her bag. She offers one to Karen. They light up.

MARGO

About Eve. I've acted pretty disgracefully toward her, too.

KAREN

Well . . .

MARGO

Let's not fumble for excuses, not here and now with my hair down. At best, let's say I've been oversensitive to . . . well, to the fact that she's so young — so feminine and helpless. To so many things I want to be for Bill . . . funny business, a woman's career. The things you drop on your way up the ladder, so you can move faster. You forget you'll need them again when you go back to being a woman. That's one career all females have in common — whether we like it or not — being a woman. Sooner or later we've got to work at it, no matter what other careers we've had or wanted . . . and, in the last analysis, nothing is any good unless you can look up just before dinner or turn around in bed — and there he is. Without that, you're not a woman. You're something with a French provincial office or a book full of clippings — but you're not a woman . . .

(she smiles at Karen)

. . . slow curtain. The end.

A pause. There are tears in Karen's eyes.

KAREN

Margo.

(she hesitates)

Margo, I want you to know how sorry I am about this . . .

MARGO

About what?

KAREN

(indicating their predicament)

This. I can't tell you how sorry I am!

MARGO

Don't give it a thought, one of destiny's merry pranks. After all, you didn't personally drain the gasoline out of the tank . . .

She snuggles down into her furs. Karen flashes an unhappy look at her. She, too, snuggles down . . .

DISSOLVE TO:

THEATRE ALLEY — NIGHT

The snow has been shoveled to either side of the alley, making a lane. The performance is just over.

Addison, his back to us, stands looking toward the stage door. A few actors, on their way out.

ADDISON'S VOICE

*Eve, of course, was superb. Many of the audience understandably preferred to return another time to see Margo. But those who remained cheered loudly, lustily and long for Eve . . . how thoughtful of her to call and invite me — that afternoon . . .*

He starts to walk toward the stage door.

ADDISON'S VOICE

*. . . and what a happy coincidence that several representatives of other newspapers happened to be present. All of us — invited that afternoon to attend an understudy's performance . . .*

He goes in the stage door.

THEATRE—BACKSTAGE

More activity than last time, the performance being just over. Addison comes through the door, picks his way toward Margo's dressing room:

ADDISON'S VOICE

*. . . about which the management knew nothing until they were forced to ring up the curtain at nine o'clock. Coincidence. Also every indication of intrigue, skulduggery and fraud . . .*

The door to the dressing room is open just a bit. Addison pauses beside the open door to listen.

BILL'S VOICE

(from within)

. . . you were better than all right, kid, you gave a performance, you rang a bell —

Addison uses his cane to swing the door open further, so that both he and we can see as well as hear.

MARGO'S DRESSING ROOM

Bill faces Eve, who wears Margo's costume. She is a ravishing sight. Her eyes shine up to his radiantly.

BILL

(continuing)

— little things here and there, it doesn't matter. You can be proud of yourself, you've got a right to be.

EVE

(quietly)

Are you proud of me, Bill?

BILL

I'll admit I was worried when Max called. I had my doubts —

EVE

You shouldn't have had any doubts.

BILL

— after all, the other day was one scene, the woods are full of one-scene sensations. But you did it. With work and patience, you'll be a fine actress. If that's what you want to be.

EVE

Is that what you want me to be?

BILL

I'm talking about you. And what you want.

EVE

So am I.

BILL

What have I got to do with it?

EVE

Everything.

BILL

(lightly)

The names I've been called. But never Svengali.

(he pats her shoulder)

Good luck.

He starts out. Addison ducks.

EVE

Don't run away, Bill.

BILL

(stops)

From what would I be running?

EVE

You're always after truth — on the stage. What about off?

BILL

(curiously)

I'm for it.

EVE

Then face it. I have. Since that first night — here — in this dressing room.

BILL

(smiles)

When I told you what every young actress should know.

EVE

When you told me that whatever I became, it would be because of you —

BILL

Your makeup's a little heavy.

EVE

— and for you.

BILL

(slowly)

You're quite a girl.

EVE

You think?

BILL

I'm in love with Margo. Hadn't you heard?

EVE

You hear all kinds of things . . .

BILL

I'm only human, rumors to the contrary. And I'm as curious as the next man . . .

EVE

Find out.

BILL

(deliberately)

Only thing, what I go after, *I* want to go after. I don't want it to come after me.

Tears come to Eve's eyes. She turns away slowly.

BILL

Don't cry. Just score it as an incomplete forward pass.

He walks out. Addison ducks to avoid being seen. Eve glares after Bill, tears the wig from her head, throws it on the dressing table. Her glance is caught by a pair of scissors. Swiftly, she snatches them up and in a sharp, vicious gesture she slashes the wig. Addison knocks politely at the door. Eve turns.

ADDISON

May I come in?

EVE

Certainly, Mr. DeWitt . . .

ADDISON

(entering)

I expected to find this little room overcrowded, with a theatre full of people at your feet . . .

EVE

I consider myself lucky they didn't throw things.

She starts creaming her face, removing makeup.

ADDISON

Of course your performance was no surprise to me. After the other day I regarded it as no more than — a promise fulfilled.

EVE

You're more than kind. But it's still Miss Channing's performance. I'm just a carbon copy you read when you can't find the original . . .

ADDISON

You're more than modest.

EVE

It's not modesty. I just don't try to kid myself.

ADDISON

A revolutionary approach to the theatre. However, if I may make a suggestion . . .

EVE

Please do.

ADDISON

I think the time has come for you to shed some of your humility. It is just as false not to blow your horn at all as it is to blow it too loudly.

EVE

I don't think I've done anything to sound off about.

ADDISON

We all come into this world with our little egos equipped with individual horns. If we don't blow them — who will?

EVE

Even so. One isolated pretty good performance by an understudy. It'll be forgotten tomorrow.

ADDISON

It needn't be.

EVE

Even if I wanted to — as you say — be less humble, blow my own horn . . . how would I do it? I'm less than nobody.

ADDISON

I am somebody.

Eve rises. She eyes him steadily.

EVE

You certainly are.

She goes into the bathroom.

ADDISON

Leave the door open a bit, so we can talk.

Eve does so.

ADDISON

After you change, if you're not busy elsewhere, we can have supper . . .

EVE

(from the bathroom)

I'd love to! Or should I pretend I'm busy?

ADDISON

(smiling)

Let's have a minimum of pretending. I'll want to do a column about you —

EVE

I'm not enough for a paragraph.

ADDISON

— perhaps more than one. There's so much I want to know. I've heard your story in bits and pieces . . . your home in Wisconsin, your tragic marriage, your fanatical attachment to Margo — it started in San Francisco, didn't it?

(No answer. Addison smiles)

I say — your idolatry of Margo started in San Francisco, didn't it?

EVE

That's right.

ADDISON

San Francisco. An oasis of civilization in the California desert. Tell me, do you share my high opinion of San Francisco?

EVE

Yes, I do.

ADDISON

And that memorable night when Margo first dazzled you from the stage — which theatre was it in San Francisco? Was it — the Shubert?

EVE

(a slight pause)

Yes. The Shubert.

ADDISON

(grins happily)

A fine old theatre, the Shubert. Full of tradition, untouched by the earthquake — so sorry — fire . . . by the way, what was your husband's name?

EVE

Eddie . . .

ADDISON

Eddie what?

Eve sticks her head and naked shoulder around the door.

EVE

I'm about to go into the shower. I won't be able to hear you . . .

ADDISON

It can wait. Where would you like to go? We'll make this a special night . . .

EVE

(trustingly)

You take charge.

ADDISON

I believe I will.

She closes the door. He leans back, lights a cigarette.

DISSOLVE TO:

52ND STREET — NEW YORK — DAY

A cab drives up to "21."

KAREN'S VOICE

*Some of the morning papers carried a little squib about Eve's performance. Not much, but full of praise . . . I couldn't imagine how they found out about it — but Lloyd said Max's publicity man probably sent out the story . . .*

Karen gets out of the cab, pays and goes in.

KAREN'S VOICE

*. . . at any rate, I felt terribly guilty and ashamed of myself — and wanted nothing so much as to forget the whole thing. Margo and I were having lunch at "21" — just like girl friends — with hats on . . .*

LOBBY — "21" — DAY

Karen consults her watch and the doorman as she enters.

KAREN

Has Miss Channing come in?

DOORMAN

Not yet, Mrs. Richards.

Karen sees Eve, who waits as Addison hands his hat, coat and cane to an attendant. She smiles, crosses to her.

KAREN

Eve. I've heard the most wonderful things about your performance —

EVE

Mostly relief that I managed to stagger through it at all.

ADDISON

She was magnificent.

KAREN

(pleased)

Then you've heard, too.

ADDISON

I was there. An eye-witness.

KAREN

(staggered)

You were there? At the play — last night?

ADDISON

(smiles)

A happy coincidence.

EVE

(quickly)

We're having lunch with a movie-talent scout.

KAREN

They certainly don't waste much time.

EVE

Nothing definite yet — it's just to have lunch.

ADDISON

They'll be wasting this much of their time at any rate. Eve has no intention of going to Hollywood.

He turns to Karen, changing the subject.

ADDISON

From the smartness of your dress, I take it your luncheon companion is a lady?

KAREN

(smiles)

Margo.

ADDISON

Margo? Lunching in public?

KAREN

It's a new Margo. But she's just as late as the old one.

ADDISON

She may be later than you think.

As he speaks, he crosses to pick up an evening paper, opens it as he comes back.

ADDISON

(handing it to her)

Why not read my column to pass the time? The minutes will fly like hours . . .

(he takes Eve's arm)

. . . and now we must join our sunburned eager beaver.

He goes up the stairs with Eve. Karen glances after them curiously, then at the column. It is headed: "Things I Promised Not to Tell" by Addison DeWitt. Her expression becomes increasingly horrified. She drops the paper and rushes out . . .

DISSOLVE TO:

MARGO'S LIVING ROOM — DAY

Addison's column quivers in Margo's hand as she strides about, reading it. Karen sits miserably.

MARGO

(declaiming)

". . . my hat which has, lo, these many seasons become more firmly rooted about my ears, is lifted to Miss Harrington. I am once more available for dancing in the streets and shouting from the housetops" . . . I thought that one went out with Woollcott . . .

(she skips part of the column)

Down here . . . here, listen to this — ". . . Miss Harrington had much to tell — and these columns shall report her faithfully — about the lamentable practice in our theatre of permitting, shall we say — mature — actresses to continue playing roles requiring a youth and vigor of which they retain but a dim memory —"

KAREN

I just can't believe it.

MARGO

It gets better! "— about the understandable reluctance on the part of our entrenched First Ladies of the Stage to encourage, shall we say — younger — actresses; about Miss Harrington's own long and unsupported struggle for opportunity —"

KAREN

I can't believe Eve said those things!

Margo crumples the paper as if it were Eve's neck.

MARGO

(pacing)

In this rat race, everybody's guilty till they're proved innocent! One of the differences between the Theatre and civilization . . .

(she hurls the paper away)

. . . what gets me is how all of the papers in town happened to catch that particular performance!

KAREN

(weakly)

Lloyd says it's a publicity release.

MARGO

The little witch must have had Indian runners out, snatching critics out of bars, steam rooms and museums or wherever they hole up . . . well, she won't get away with it! Nor will Addison DeWitt and his poison pen! If Equity or my lawyer can't or won't do anything about it, I will personally stuff that pathetic little lost lamb down Mr. DeWitt's ugly throat . . .

She pauses in mid-air to look at . . . Bill. He has come up the stairs two at a time, stands at the landing.

BILL

(quietly)

I came as soon as I read that piece of filth. I ran all the way . . .

Margo suddenly starts to cry. She turns from him. Bill takes her in his arms. He holds her . . .

BILL

Bill's here, baby. Everything's all right, now.

Margo says nothing, just hides in his embrace. He soothes her, pets her . . . he looks over at Karen.

KAREN

I guess at this point I'm what the French call de trop . . .

BILL

(smiles)

Maybe just a little around the edges.

Karen smiles back, waves, and goes out.

DISSOLVE TO:

RICHARDS' APARTMENT — DAY

Karen's having some lunch. Lloyd, still in his robe, sits opposite her having some coffee and a cigarette. A copy of the interview before them.

LLOYD

(is saying)

— it's Addison, from start to finish, it drips with his brand of venom . . . taking advantage of a kid like that, twisting her words, making her say what he wanted her to say —

KAREN

Where'd you get all that information?

LLOYD

(puts out his cigarette)

Eve.

KAREN

Eve?

LLOYD

She's been to see me, as a matter of fact she left just before you came in — you just missed her.

KAREN

That was a pity . . .

LLOYD

(gets up)

She wanted to explain about the interview, wanted to apologize to someone — and didn't dare face Margo . . .

KAREN

I wonder why.

Lloyd wanders about — he seems to be searching for words, for a position to maintain . . .

LLOYD

She started to tell me all about it — and she couldn't finish, she cried so . . .

He's over by a window, his back to her. Karen eyes him curiously, waiting for the payoff.

LLOYD

(finally)

You know, I've been going over our financial condition — if you'll pardon the expression.

KAREN

That's quite a change of subject.

LLOYD

(walks again)

What with taxes coming up — and since I'm a playwright and not an oil-well operator — well, I've been thinking . . .

KAREN

I'm trying hard to follow you.

LLOYD

If — instead of waiting until next season to do *Footsteps on the Ceiling,* which is in pretty good shape — and if Margo can be talked into going on tour with *Aged in Wood* — we could put *Footsteps* into production right away . . .

KAREN

I'm beginning to catch up.

LLOYD

If we could cast it properly, that is . . .

KAREN

(carefully)

Maybe get some younger actress for the part? Someone who'd look the part as well as play it?

LLOYD

(smiles)

You've got to admit it would be a novelty.

KAREN

Now you're quoting Addison. Or Eve.

A pause.

LLOYD

Eve did mention the play, you know. But just in

passing — she'd never ask to play a part like "Cora." She'd never have the nerve . . .

KAREN

Eve would ask Abbott to give her Costello.

LLOYD

No, I got the idea myself — while she was talking to me . . .

KAREN

With gestures, of course.

LLOYD

(wistfully)

For once, to write something and have it realized completely. For once, not to compromise —

Now Karen explodes. She rises.

KAREN

Lloyd Richards, you are not to consider giving that contemptible little worm the part of "Cora"!

LLOYD

Now just a minute —

KAREN

Margo Channing has not been exactly a compromise all these years. Half the playwrights in the world would give their shirts for that particular compromise!

LLOYD

(angry)

Now just a minute!

KAREN

It strikes me that Eve's disloyalty and ingratitude must be contagious!

Lloyd's full of anger and guilt. He snaps back.

LLOYD

All this fuss and hysteria because an impulsive kid got carried away by excitement and the conniving of a professional manure slinger named DeWitt! She apologized, didn't she?

KAREN

On her knees, I have no doubt! Very touching, very Academy-of-Dramatic-Arts!

LLOYD

That bitter cynicism of yours is something you've acquired since you left Radcliffe!

KAREN

The cynicism you refer to, I acquired the day I discovered I was different from little boys!

THE PHONE HAS BEEN RINGING. Lloyd snarls into it.

LLOYD

Hello!

(he quiets down)

. . . hi, Margo . . . no, not at all, Karen and I were just chatting . . . hmm? . . . why — why, yes, I'm sure we can and I'm sure we'd love to . . . right . . . 11:45ish. See you then . . .

He hangs up. He smiles — suddenly, there's peace.

LLOYD

Margo — and Bill — want us to meet them at the Cub Room tonight, after theatre. For a bottle of wine.

KAREN

(smiles)

Margo in the Cub Room. I couldn't be more surprised if she'd said Grant's Tomb.

LLOYD

I'm glad Bill's back.

KAREN

They'd die without each other.

A pause.

LLOYD

Darling, I didn't promise Eve anything. Just said I thought she'd be fine for the part, but there were some practical difficulties . . .

KAREN

Such as?

LLOYD

(grins)

You — for one. I told her you were set on Margo playing the part — and that I certainly wouldn't make a change without your approval . . .

Karen smiles happily.

KAREN

That's fine. Fine and dandy. I'd enjoy nothing more. Just refer all of Miss Harrington's future requests to me . . .

DISSOLVE TO:

CUB ROOM — STORK CLUB — NIGHT

Margo, Karen, Bill and Lloyd are ensconced happily at a table in the rear of the room. A bottle of fine wine is being poured. Their mood is equally bubbly.

BILL

The so-called art of acting is not one for which I have a particularly high regard . . .

MARGO

Hear, hear.

BILL

But you may quote me as follows. Quote. Tonight Miss Margo Channing gave a performance in your cockamaimy play, the like of which I have never seen before and expect rarely to see again. Unquote.

MARGO

He does not exaggerate. I was good.

BILL

You were great.

As they look at each other, they reflect the understanding that has hit them both at last.

LLOYD

It's been quite a night. I understand that your understudy — a Miss Harrington — has given her notice.

MARGO

(eyes still on Bill)

Too bad.

BILL

(eyes still on Margo)

I'm broken up about it . . .

The wine has been poured by now.

LLOYD

For some reason you can't just pick up champagne and drink it. Somebody's got to be very witty about a toast.

(he lifts his glass)

For instance . . .

BILL

(abruptly)

I'm going to propose the toast. Without wit. With all my heart.

Lloyd lowers his glass. There's a little pause.

BILL

To Margo. To my bride-to-be.

MARGO

Glory hallelujah.

LLOYD

Well of all —

KAREN

Margo!

BILL

Drink.

They drink, then burst into a flurry of questions.

KAREN

When? When are you going to do it?

BILL

Tomorrow we meet at City Hall at ten —
(to Margo)
— and you're going to be on time.

MARGO

Yes, sir.

LLOYD

City Hall, that's for prize fighters, and reporters —
I see a cathedral, a bishop, banks of flowers . . .

BILL

It's only for the license. There's a three-day wait — blood tests, things like that . . .

MARGO

I'll marry you if it turns out you've got no blood at all.

KAREN

(to Margo)

What are you going to wear?

MARGO

Something simple. A fur coat over a nightgown.

BILL

The point is — in a cathedral, a ball park or a penny arcade — we want to have you two beside us as our nearest and dearest friends . . .

KAREN

. . . which we are. Which we'll always be.

Lloyd fills all the glasses.

LLOYD

There are very few moments in life as good as this. Let's remember it.

(he lifts his glass)

To each of us and all of us . . . never have we been more close — may we never be further apart.

They drink. A waiter approaches with a note.

WAITER

Mrs. Richards?

KAREN

Yes?

WAITER

For you.

Karen stares at it curiously, then opens it.

LLOYD

Very indiscreet. A note right out in the open like that. Next time tell your lover to blow smoke rings — or tap a glass . . .

MARGO

Lloyd, I want you to be big about this . . . the world is full of love tonight, no woman is safe.

KAREN

(angrily)

This beats all world's records for running, standing and jumping gall!

She whips the note to Margo, who reads it aloud:

MARGO

(reading)

"Please forgive me for butting into what seems such a happy occasion — but it's most important that I speak with you. Please" — it's underlined — "meet me in the ladies' room. Eve."

BILL

I understand she is now the understudy in there.

MARGO

(looking about)

Pass me that empty bottle. I may find her . . . why, look. There's Rasputin.

THEIR VIEWPOINT

Addison sits near the entrance, at a banquette table for two. A crumpled napkin and a wine glass indicate Eve's place. He nibbles daintily at some blini.

THE GROUP

Margo hails a passing captain.

MARGO

Encore du champagne.

CAPTAIN

More champagne, Miss Channing?

MARGO

That's what I said, bub.

LLOYD

(to Karen)

After all, maybe she just wants to apologize.

KAREN

I have no possible interest in anything she'd have to say.

BILL

But what *could* she say? That's what fascinates me.

LLOYD

Go on — find out.

MARGO

Karen, in all the years of our friendship, I have never let you go to the ladies' room alone. But now I must. I am busting to know what goes on in that feverish little brain waiting in there . . .

KAREN

Well . . . all right.

She gets up and goes. The CAMERA takes her past Addison's table. He rises in polite surprise.

ADDISON

Karen! How nice.

She walks past him without a word. He smiles, looks toward the group. He raises his glass in a toast.

GROUP

Margo responds to the toast by waving an onion with a grand flourish, then eating it.

BILL

Very effective. But why take it out on me?

He eats one in self-defense.

LADIES' ROOM — STORK CLUB

Never having been there, I can't say what it looks like. It is to be hoped that there is an outer and inner room. We are concerned with the outer.

There is an attendant in charge, and a constantly changing flow of ladies who pause to make various repairs.

There are two chairs — or a banquette — in a corner. Eve waits there. She rises as Karen approaches.

EVE

I was wondering whether you'd come at all.

KAREN

Don't get up.

(she smiles grimly)

And don't act as if I were the queen mother.

EVE

I don't expect you to be pleasant.

KAREN

I don't intend to be.

EVE

Can't we sit down? Just for a minute.

She sits. Karen remains standing.

EVE

I've got a lot to say. And none of it is easy.

KAREN

There can't be very much —

EVE

Oh, but there is —

KAREN

— and easy or not, I won't believe a word.

EVE

Why should you?

(a pause)

Please sit down.

Karen sits, reluctantly and rigidly.

EVE

You know, I've always considered myself a very clever girl. Smart. Good head on my shoulders, that sort of thing, never the wrong word at the wrong time . . . but then, I'd never met Addison DeWitt.

(another pause)

I remember once I had a tooth pulled. They gave me some anaesthetic — I don't remember the name — and it affected me in a strange way. I heard myself saying things I wasn't even thinking . . . as if my mind were some place outside of my body, and couldn't control what I did or said —

KAREN

(leading her on)

— and you felt just like that talking to Addison.

EVE

(nods)

In a way. You find yourself trying to say what you mean, but somehow the words change — and they become his words — and suddenly you're not saying what you mean, but what he means —

KAREN

(sharply)

Do you expect me to believe that you didn't say any of those things — that they were all Addison?

EVE

No! I don't expect you to believe anything. Except that the responsibility is mine. And the disgrace.

KAREN

Let's not get over-dramatic.

EVE

(smiles grimly)

You've really got a low opinion of me, haven't you? Well, I'll give you some pleasant news. I've been told off in no uncertain terms all over town. Miss Channing should be happy to hear that. To know how loyal her friends are — how much more loyal they are than she had a right to expect me to be.

She turns away from Karen. Karen's embarrassed.

KAREN

Eve . . . don't cry.

EVE

(turned away)

I'm not crying.

KAREN

Tell me. How did your lunch turn out — with the man from Hollywood?

EVE

Some vague promises of a test, that's all — if a particular part should come along, one of those things —

KAREN

But the raves about your performance —

EVE

— an understudy's performance.

KAREN

Well. I think you're painting the picture a little blacker than it is, really. If nothing else — and don't underestimate him — you have a powerful friend in Addison.

EVE

He's not my friend. You were my friends.

KAREN

He can help you.

EVE

I wish I'd never met him, I'd like him to be dead . . . I want my friends back.

This time she does cry. Softly, miserably. Karen looks about. A pause. She puts an arm around Eve.

KAREN

Eve. I — I don't think you meant to cause unhappiness. But you did. More to yourself, perhaps — as it turned out — than to anyone else.

EVE

I'll never get over it.

KAREN

(smiles)

Yes, you will. You Theatre people always do. Nothing is forever in the Theatre. Love or hate, success or failure — whatever it is, it's here, it flares up and burns hot — and then it's gone.

EVE

I wish I could believe that.

KAREN

Give yourself time. Don't worry too much about

what people think. You're very young and very talented . . .

(she gets up, her hand still on Eve's shoulder)

. . . and, believe it or not, if there's anything I can do —

Eve has reached up to take Karen's hand. She holds it now, as she turns slowly to face her.

EVE

There is something.

Karen stares down at her. Eve's eyes burn into hers. Karen is caught, fascinated by them.

KAREN

I think I know . . .

EVE

Something most important you can do.

KAREN

You want to play "Cora." You want me to tell Lloyd I think you should play it.

EVE

If you told him so, he'd give me the part. He said he would.

KAREN

After all you've said . . . don't you know that part was written for Margo?

EVE

It could have been — fifteen years ago. It's my part, now.

KAREN

You talk just as Addison said you did.

EVE

"Cora" is my part. You've got to tell Lloyd it's for me.

KAREN

I don't think anything in the world could make me say that.

She turns away again, but Eve's grip is like a vise.

EVE

Addison wants me to play it.

KAREN

Over my dead body.

EVE

(cold, relentless)

That won't be necessary. Addison knows how Margo happened to miss that performance — how I happened to know she'd miss it in time to call him and notify every paper in town . . .

(Karen stops struggling)

. . . it's quite a story. Addison could make quite

a thing of it — imagine how snide and vicious he could get and still write nothing but the truth. I had a time persuading him . . .

(she smiles, now)

. . . you'd better sit down. You look a bit wobbly.

(Karen sits)

If I play "Cora," Addison will never tell what happened — in or out of print. A simple exchange of favors. And I'm so happy I can do something for you — at long last.

(Karen covers her face with her hands)

Your friendship with Margo — your deep, close friendship — what would happen to it, do you think, if she knew the cheap trick you'd played on her — for my benefit? And you and Lloyd — how long, even in the Theatre, before people forgot what happened — and trusted you again?

(now Eve gets up)

No . . . it would be so much easier on everyone concerned, if I were to play "Cora." And so much better Theatre, too . . .

Karen looks up slowly.

KAREN

A part in a play. You'd do all that — just for a part in a play.

EVE

(smiles)

I'd do much more — for a part that good.

She leaves. Karen is alone.

CUB ROOM — NIGHT

Eve enters and slides in beside Addison.

ADDISON

Hungry?

EVE

Just some coffee.

ADDISON

(pours)

I'm not surprised. After eating so much humble pie.

EVE

Nothing of the kind. Karen and I had a nice talk.

ADDISON

Heart to heart? Woman to woman? Including a casual reference to the part of "Cora" — and your hopes of playing it?

EVE

I discussed it very openly. I told her that I had spoken to Lloyd — and that he was interested.

ADDISON

She mentioned, of course, that Margo expects to play the part?

EVE

Oddly enough — she didn't say a word about Margo. Just that she'll be happy to do what she can to see that I play the part.

Addison puffs at his cigarette, bemused.

ADDISON

Just like that, eh?

EVE

Just like that.

ADDISON

(thoughtfully)

Do you know, Eve — sometimes I think you keep things from me.

Eve's feelings are hurt.

EVE

I don't think that's funny.

ADDISON

It wasn't meant to be.

EVE

I confide in you and rely on you more than anyone I've ever known! To say a thing like that now

—without any reason—when I need you more than ever . . .

ADDISON

(breaks in)

I hope you mean what you say, Eve. I intend to hold you to it.

Their eyes meet.

ADDISON

We have a great deal in common, it seems to me.

They both look up as Karen passes them on her way back to her table.

GROUP

as Karen joins them. Another bottle of champagne has come and almost gone—there's a fine, cheery feeling among them. Margo, in particular, is cheery. A pause. Karen downs a glass of champagne.

LLOYD

Well? What happened?

KAREN

Nothing much. She apologized.

MARGO

With tears?

KAREN

With tears.

MARGO

But not right away? First the business of fighting them off, chin-up, stout fella . . .

KAREN

Check.

MARGO

Very classy stuff, lots of technique —

LLOYD

You mean — all this time — she's done nothing but apologize? What'd you say?

KAREN

Not much.

MARGO

Groom —

(Bill says "Huh?")

— may I have a wedding present?

BILL

What would you like? Texas?

MARGO

I want everybody to shut up about Eve. Just shut up about Eve, that's all I want. Give Karen more wine . . .

(blissfully)

. . . never have I been so happy. Isn't this a lovely

room? The Cub Room. What a lovely, clever name. Where the elite meet. Never have I seen so much elite — and all with their eyes on me. Waiting for me to crack that little gnome over the noggin with a bottle. But not tonight. I'm forgiving tonight. Even Eve. I forgive Eve . . . there they go.

They all look.

ADDISON AND EVE

They get up and go without looking back.

GROUP

They watch for an instant.

MARGO

There goes Eve. Eve evil, little Miss Evil. But the evil that men do — how does it go, groom? Something about the good they leave behind — I played it once in rep in Wilkes-Barre . . .

BILL

You've got it backwards. Even for Wilkes-Barre.

MARGO

Do you know why I forgive Eve? Because she left good behind — the four of us, together like this. It's Eve's fault — I forgive her . . .

KAREN's reactions are, of course, most important. Knowing what she's done to Margo — wondering how to do what she must.

MARGO

. . . and Bill. Especially Bill. Eve did that, too.

LLOYD

You know, she probably means well after all.

MARGO

She is a louse.

BILL

(to Lloyd)

Never try to outguess Margo.

MARGO

Groom.

BILL

Yes, dear.

MARGO

You know what I'm going to be?

BILL

A cowboy.

MARGO

A married lady.

BILL

With a paper to prove it.

MARGO

I'm going to have a home. Not just a house I'm afraid to stay in . . . and a man to go with it. I'll look up at six o'clock — and there he'll be . . . remember, Karen?

KAREN

(quietly)

I remember.

MARGO

(to Bill)

You'll be there, won't you?

BILL

(grins)

Often enough to keep the franchise.

MARGO

A foursquare, upright, downright, forthright married lady . . . that's for me. And no more make believe! Off stage or on . . . remember, Lloyd?

(Lloyd nods)

I mean it, now. Grown-up women only, I might even play a mother — only one child, of course, and not over eight . . .

(they all smile)

Lloyd, will you promise not to be angry with me?

LLOYD

(smiles)

That depends.

MARGO

I mean really, deeply angry.

LLOYD

I don't think I could be.

MARGO

Well. I don't want to play "Cora."

KAREN

(explodes)

What?

Margo misinterprets her vehemence.

MARGO

(hastily)

Now wait a minute, you're always so touchy about his plays, it isn't the part — it's a great part. And a fine play. But not for me any more — not a four-square, upright, downright, forthright married lady . . .

LLOYD

What's your being married got to do with it?

MARGO

It means I've finally got a life to live! I don't have to play parts I'm too old for — just because I've got nothing to do with my nights!

(then quietly)

I know you've made plans. I'll make it up to you, believe me. I'll tour a year with this one, anything — only you do understand — don't you, Lloyd?

Lloyd never gets to answer. Because Karen, before anyone can stop her, is lost in hysterical laughter . . .

LLOYD

What's so funny?

KAREN

Nothing.

BILL

Nothing?

KAREN

Everything . . . everything's so funny . . .

Margo removes the champagne glass from in front of Karen.

FADE OUT

FADE IN

THEATRE — A SILENT SCENE

Karen is seated unobtrusively in a rear lower box. Lloyd sits beside Max up front.

On stage, the play is "on its feet." Eve plays a dramatic scene with a young man. They carry "sides" but do not consult them.

As she speaks, Eve moves upstage, turns to face the young man who is forced to turn his back to the auditorium.

Bill calls a halt. He indicates to Eve that she was to have remained downstage.

Eve seems to be at a loss. She looks at Lloyd.

Lloyd rises, says that he told her to make the change.

Bill comes down to the footlights to tell him to stick to writing, he'll do the directing. It mounts swiftly to a screaming fight. Bill throws the script out into the auditorium, takes his coat and stalks off.

Eve runs after him. Max retrieves the script. Lloyd remains adamant. Karen has risen in dismay.

Eve drags Bill back. Without looking at Lloyd, he takes

the script from Max, tells the actors to pick up where they left off.

Eve whispers to Lloyd from the stage. Lloyd smiles, mollified, sits down again with Max.

Karen walks up the side aisle, out of the theatre . . .

KAREN'S VOICE

*Lloyd never got around, somehow — to asking whether it was all right with me for Eve to play "Cora" . . .*

*Bill, oddly enough, refused to direct the play at first — with Eve in it. Lloyd and Max finally won him over . . . Margo never came to a rehearsal — too much to do around the house, she said. I'd never known Bill and Lloyd to fight as bitterly and often . . . and always over some business for Eve, or a move or the way she read a speech . . . but then I'd never known Lloyd to meddle as much with Bill's directing — as far as it affected Eve, that is . . . somehow, Eve kept them going. Bill stuck it out — and Lloyd seemed happy — and I thought it might be best if I skipped rehearsals from then on . . .*

DISSOLVE TO:

RICHARDS' BEDROOM — NIGHT

It is a lovely, large room. Two double beds, *not* alongside each other and each with an extension phone beside it. In addition to the door to the living room, there are two more — to separate dressing rooms and baths.

Lloyd is asleep. But not Karen. She turns restlessly, finally sits up, lights a cigarette.

KAREN'S VOICE

*It seemed to me I had known always that it would happen — and here it was. I felt helpless, that helplessness you feel when you have no talent to offer — outside of loving your husband. How could I compete? Everything Lloyd loved about me, he had gotten used to long ago . . .*

The phone jangles suddenly, startling her. It wakes Lloyd up. Karen answers.

KAREN

Hello . . . who? . . . who's calling Mr. Richards?

ROOMING HOUSE — NIGHT

A girl, in a wrapper, at a wall phone. Her hair's in curlers. She's frightened.

GIRL

My name wouldn't mean anything. I room across the hall from Eve Harrington, and she isn't well.

She's been crying all night and hysterical, and she doesn't want a doctor . . .

RICHARDS' BEDROOM

Lloyd is sitting on the edge of the bed, looking over . . .

LLOYD

Who is it? What's it all about?

KAREN

(into phone)

Did Miss Harrington tell you to call Mr. Richards?

Lloyd picks up his phone.

ROOMING HOUSE

GIRL

No, Eve didn't say to call him, but I remembered I saw Mr. Richards with her a couple of times — and I thought they being such good friends . . .

RICHARDS' BEDROOM

LLOYD

(into phone)

Hello . . . hello, this is Lloyd Richards. Where is Eve? Let me talk to her —

ROOMING HOUSE

GIRL

She's up in her room, Mr. Richards. I really hate

to bother you like this, but the way Eve's been feeling — I'm just worried sick what with her leaving for New Haven tomorrow, and everything . . .

RICHARDS' BEDROOM

LLOYD

Tell her not to worry — tell her I'll be right over.

ROOMING HOUSE

GIRL

I'll tell her, Mr. Richards.

She hangs up. As she moves from the phone, the ANGLE WIDENS to disclose Eve at the foot of the stairs. The girls smile at each other. They go upstairs, arm in arm.

RICHARDS' BEDROOM

Karen is still in bed, phone still in her hand. She hangs up, swings her legs out, puts out her cigarette, gets into a robe. The open door and light of his dressing room tell us where Lloyd is.

Karen walks to the door, starts to say something, changes her mind. She crosses to a table, lights a fresh cigarette, comes back to the door.

KAREN

(finally)

Aren't you . . . broadening the duties of a playwright just a bit? Rushing off in the middle of the night — like a country doctor?

No answer except the opening and closing of drawers.

KAREN

What would you do if, instead of Eve, the leading man had called up to say he was hysterical?

Still no answer. Her tension increasing, Karen goes back to the table, snubs out the fresh cigarette, then strides swiftly back to the open door.

KAREN

Lloyd, I don't want you to go!

Now Lloyd appears. He's in flannels, and a sport shirt with no tie. He's confused and guilty and tortured.

LLOYD

I didn't think you would! It seems to me, Karen, that for some time, now, you've been developing a deep unconcern for the feelings of human beings in general —

KAREN

I'm a human being, I've got some!

LLOYD

(goes right on)

— and for my feelings in particular! For my play,

my career — and now for a frightened, hysterical girl on the eve of her first night in the theatre!

He goes back into his room.

KAREN

Have you forgotten about Eve? What she is, what she's done?

LLOYD

(from the room)

Old wives' tales, born of envy and jealousy! And a phobia against truth!

KAREN

Then tell me this isn't true! That your concern for your play and career is one thing — and that poor frightened hysterical girl is another — and that your concern for her has nothing to do with either your play or your career!

Lloyd comes out wearing a jacket. He crosses to the door, Karen after him.

KAREN

That first, last and foremost — your reason for going now is that you want to be with Eve! Three in the morning or high noon — play or no play — wife or no wife!

(Lloyd stops at the door)

Isn't it true, Lloyd?

Lloyd goes out. Karen looks after him, despairing.

DISSOLVE TO:

SHUBERT THEATRE — NEW HAVEN — DAY

The theatre is but a few doors from the TAFT HOTEL. The marquee announces a new play by Lloyd Richards, presented by Max Fabian, opening tonight.

Addison and Eve stand before the theatre admiring her photo on a lobby display. None of the actors is starred.

ADDISON'S VOICE

*To the Theatre world — New Haven, Connecticut, is a short stretch of sidewalk between the Shubert Theatre and the Taft Hotel, surrounded by what looks very much like a small city. It is here that managers have what are called out-of-town openings — which are openings for New Yorkers who want to go out of town.*

They start for the hotel — Eve's arm through Addison's.

CLOSER

as they walk.

EVE

What a day — what a heavenly day.

ADDISON

D-day.

EVE

Just like it.

ADDISON

And tomorrow morning, you will have won your beachhead on the shores of Immortality.

EVE

(grins)

Stop rehearsing your column . . . isn't it strange, Addison? I thought I'd be panic-stricken, want to run away or something. Instead, I can't wait for tonight to come. To come and go.

ADDISON

Are you that sure of tomorrow?

EVE

Aren't you?

ADDISON

Frankly — yes.

They've arrived in front of the hotel.

EVE

It'll be a night to remember. It'll bring to me everything I've ever wanted. The end of an old road — and the beginning of a new one.

ADDISON

All paved with diamonds and gold?

EVE

You know me better than that.

ADDISON

Paved with what, then?

EVE

Stars.

She goes in. Addison follows her.

DISSOLVE TO:

CORRIDOR — TAFT HOTEL — DAY

Addison accompanies Eve along the corridor to her door.

EVE

What time?

ADDISON

Almost four.

EVE

Plenty of time for a nice long nap — we rehearsed most of last night . . .

ADDISON

You could sleep, too, couldn't you?

EVE

Why not?

They've arrived at her door. She opens it.

ADDISON

The mark of a true killer.

(he holds out his hand)

Sleep tight, rest easy — and come out fighting . . .

EVE

Why'd you call me a killer?

ADDISON

Did I say killer? I meant champion. I get my boxing terms mixed.

He turns to go. After a few steps —

EVE

(calling)

Addison —

(he pauses)

— come on in for just a minute, won't you? There's . . . I've got something to tell you.

Addison turns curiously, and enters behind her.

EVE'S SUITE — TAFT HOTEL — DAY

Old-fashioned, dreary and small. The action starts in the living room and continues to the bedroom.

Addison closes the door, crosses to a comfortable chair.

ADDISON

Suites are for expense accounts. Aren't you being extravagant?

EVE

Max is paying for it. He and Lloyd had a terrific row but Lloyd insisted . . . well. Can I fix you a drink?

She indicates a table elaborately stocked with liquor, glasses, etc. Addison's eyebrows lift.

ADDISON

Also with the reluctant compliments of Max Fabian?

EVE

Lloyd. I never have any, and he likes a couple of drinks after we finish — so he sent it up . . .

ADDISON

Some plain soda.

(Eve starts to fix it)

Lloyd must be expecting a record run in New Haven.

EVE

That's for tonight. You're invited. We're having everyone up after the performance.

ADDISON

We're?

EVE

Lloyd and I.

She carries the soda to him, sits on an ottoman at his feet.

ADDISON

I find it odd that Karen isn't here for the opening, don't you?

He sips his soda and puts it away, carefully avoiding a look at Eve. As he looks back —

EVE

Addison . . .

ADDISON

(blandly)

She's always been so fanatically devoted to Lloyd. I would imagine that only death or destruction could keep her —

EVE

(breaks in)

Addison, just a few minutes ago. When I told you this would be a night to remember — that it would bring to me everything I wanted —

ADDISON

(nods)

— something about an old road ending and a new one starting — paved with stars . . .

EVE

I didn't mean just the theatre.

ADDISON

What else?

Eve gets up, crosses to look out over the Common.

EVE

(her back to him)

Lloyd Richards. He's going to leave Karen. We're going to be married.

For just a flash, Addison's eyes narrow coldly, viciously. Then they crinkle into a bland smile.

ADDISON

So that's it. Lloyd. Still just the theatre after all . . .

EVE

(turns, shocked)

It's nothing of the kind! Lloyd loves me, I love him!

ADDISON

I know nothing about Lloyd and his loves — I leave those to Louisa May Alcott. But I do know you . . .

EVE

I'm in love with Lloyd!

ADDISON

Lloyd Richards is commercially the most successful playwright in America —

EVE

You have no right to say such things!

ADDISON

— and artistically, the most promising! Eve dear, this is Addison.

Eve drops her shocked manner like a cape. Her face lights up — she crosses back to the ottoman.

EVE

Addison, won't it be just perfect? Lloyd and I —

there's no telling how far we can go . . . he'll write great plays for me, I'll make them be great!

(as she sits)

You're the only one I've told, the only one that knows except Lloyd and me . . .

ADDISON

. . . and Karen.

EVE

She doesn't know.

ADDISON

She knows enough not to be here.

EVE

But not all of it — not that Lloyd and I are going to be married . . .

ADDISON

(thoughtfully)

I see. And when was this unholy alliance joined?

EVE

We decided the night before last, before we came up here . . .

ADDISON

(increasingly tense)

Was the setting properly romantic — the lights on dimmers, gypsy violins off stage?

EVE

The setting wasn't romantic, but Lloyd was. He woke me up at three in the morning, banging on my door — he couldn't sleep, he told me — he'd left Karen, he couldn't go on with the play or anything else until I promised to marry him . . . we sat and talked until it was light. He never went home . . .

ADDISON

You sat and talked until it was light . . .

EVE

(meaningly)

We sat and talked, Addison. I want a run-of-the-play contract.

ADDISON

(quietly)

There never was, there'll never be another like you.

EVE

(happily)

Well, say something — anything! Congratulations, skoal — good work, Eve!

Addison rises slowly, to his full height. As Eve watches him, as her eyes go up to his, her smile fades —

ADDISON

(slowly)

What do you take me for?

EVE

(cautiously)

I don't know that I take you for anything . . .

ADDISON

(moving away)

Is it possible — even conceivable — that you've confused me with that gang of backward children you've been playing tricks on? That you have the same contempt for me that you have for them?

EVE

I'm sure you mean something by that, Addison — but I don't know what.

ADDISON

Look closely, Eve, it's time you did. I am Addison DeWitt. I am nobody's fool. Least of all — yours.

EVE

I never intended you to be.

ADDISON

Yes, you did. You still do.

Eve gets up, now.

EVE

I still don't know what you're getting at. Right now I want to take my nap. It's important that I—

ADDISON

(breaks in)

— it's important right now that we talk. Killer to killer.

EVE

(wisely)

Champion to champion.

ADDISON

Not with me, you're no champion. You're stepping way up in class.

EVE

Addison, will you please say what you have to say plainly and distinctly — and then get out so I can take my nap!

ADDISON

Very well, plainly and distinctly. Although I consider it unnecessary — because you know as well as I, what I am about to say . . .

(they are now facing each other)

Lloyd may leave Karen, but he will not leave Karen for you.

EVE

What do you mean by that?

ADDISON

More plainly and more distinctly? I have not come to New Haven to see the play, discuss your dreams, or to pull the ivy from the walls of Yale! I have come to tell you that you will not marry Lloyd — or anyone else — because I will not permit it.

EVE

What have you got to do with it?

ADDISON

Everything. Because after tonight, you will belong to me.

EVE

I can't believe my ears . . .

ADDISON

A dull cliché.

EVE

Belong — to you? That sounds medieval — something out of an old melodrama . . .

ADDISON

So does the history of the world for the past twenty years. I don't enjoy putting it as bluntly as this, frankly I had hoped that you would, somehow, have known — have taken it for granted that you and I . . .

EVE

. . . taken it for granted? That you and I . . .

She smiles. Then she chuckles, then laughs. A mistake. Addison slaps her sharply across the face.

ADDISON

(quietly)

Remember as long as you live, never to laugh at me. At anything or anyone else — but never at me.

Eve eyes him coldly, goes to the door, throws it open.

EVE

Get out!

Addison walks to the door, closes it.

ADDISON

You're too short for that gesture. Besides, it went out with Mrs. Fiske.

EVE

Then if you won't get out, I'll have you thrown out.

She goes to the phone.

ADDISON

Don't pick it up! Don't even put your hand on it.

She doesn't. Her back is to him. Addison smiles.

ADDISON

Something told you to do as I say, didn't it? That instinct is worth millions, you can't buy it, cherish it, Eve. When that alarm goes off, go to your battle stations.

He comes up behind her. Eve is tense and wary.

ADDISON

Your name is not Eve Harrington. It is Gertrude Slescynski.

EVE

What of it?

ADDISON

It is true that your parents were poor. They still are. And they would like to know how you are — and where. They haven't heard from you for three years . . .

EVE

(curtly)

What of it?

She walks away. Addison eyes her keenly.

ADDISON

A matter of opinion. Granted. It is also true that you worked in a brewery. But life in the brewery was apparently not as dull as you pictured it. As a matter of fact it got less and less dull — until your boss's wife had your boss followed by detectives!

EVE

(whirls on him)

She never proved anything, not a thing!

ADDISON

But the $500 you got to get out of town brought you straight to New York — didn't it?

Eve turns and runs into the bedroom, slamming the door. Addison opens it, follows close after her . . . He can be seen in the bedroom, shouting at Eve who is *offscene.*

ADDISON

That $500 brought you straight to New York — didn't it?

BEDROOM

Eve, trapped, in a corner of the room.

EVE

She was a liar, she was a liar!

ADDISON

Answer my question! Weren't you paid to get out of town?

Eve throws herself on the bed, face down, bursts into tears. Addison, merciless, moves closer.

ADDISON

There was no Eddie — no pilot — and you've never been married! That was not only a lie, but an insult to dead heroes and to the women who loved them . . .

(Eve, sobbing, puts her hands over her ears. Addison, closer, pulls them away)

San Francisco has no Shubert Theatre, you've never been to San Francisco! That was a stupid lie, easy to expose, not worthy of you . . .

Eve twists to look up at him, her eyes streaming.

EVE

I had to get in, to meet Margo! I had to say something, be somebody, make her like me!

ADDISON

She did like you, she helped and trusted you! You paid her back by trying to take Bill away!

EVE

That's not true!

ADDISON

I was there, I saw you and heard you through the dressing-room door!

Eve turns face down again, sobbing miserably.

ADDISON

You used my name and my column to blackmail Karen into getting you the part of "Cora" — and you lied to me about it!

EVE

(into the bed)

No — no — no . . .

ADDISON

I had lunch with Karen not three hours ago. As always with women who want to find out things, she told more than she learned . . .

(he lets go of her hands)

. . . do you want to change your story about Lloyd beating at your door the other night?

Eve covers her face with her hands.

EVE

Please . . . please . . .

Addison gets off the bed, looks down at her.

ADDISON

That I should want you at all suddenly strikes me as the height of improbability. But that, in itself, is probably the reason. You're an improbable person, Eve, and so am I. We have that in common. Also a contempt for humanity, an inability to love or be loved, insatiable ambition — and talent. We deserve each other. Are you listening to me?

Eve lies listlessly now, her tear-stained cheek against the coverlet. She nods.

ADDISON

Then say so.

EVE

Yes, Addison.

ADDISON

And you realize — you agree how completely you belong to me?

EVE

Yes, Addison.

ADDISON

Take your nap, now. And good luck for tonight.

He starts out.

EVE

(tonelessly)

I won't play tonight.

(Addison pauses)

I couldn't. Not possibly. I couldn't go on . . .

ADDISON

(smiles)

Couldn't go on? You'll give the performance of your life.

He goes out. The CAMERA REMAINS on Eve's forlorn, tear-stained face. Her eyes close . . . she goes to sleep.

DISSOLVE THROUGH TO:

DINING HALL — SARAH SIDDONS SOCIETY

THE STOPPED ACTION of Eve reaching out for the award. The applause and bulb-popping still going on.

ADDISON'S VOICE

*And she gave the performance of her life. And it was a night to remember, that night . . .*

THE ACTION picks up where it left off. Eve accepts the award from the aged actor, kisses him tenderly, folds the award to her bosom and waits for quiet.

She speaks with assurance, yet modestly and humbly.

EVE

Honored members of the Sarah Siddons Society, distinguished guests, ladies and gentlemen: What is there for me to say? Everything wise and witty has long since been said — by minds more mature and talents far greater than mine. For me to thank you as equals would be presumptuous — I am an apprentice in the Theatre and have much to learn from all of you. I can say only that I am proud and happy and that I regard this great honor not so much as an award for what I have achieved, but as a standard to hold against what I have yet to accomplish.

(applause)

And further, I regard it as bestowed upon me only in part. The larger share belongs to my friends in the Theatre — and to the Theatre itself, which has given me all I have. In good conscience, I must give credit where credit is due. To Max Fabian —

MAX

He sits erect, beaming proudly.

EVE'S VOICE

— dear Max. Dear, sentimental, generous, courageous Max Fabian — who took a chance on an unknown, untried, amateur . . .

EVE

After applause greets Max.

EVE

And to my first friend in the Theatre — whose kindness and graciousness I shall never forget . . . Karen — Mrs. Lloyd Richards . . .

KAREN

Resumes her doodling as applause breaks out for her . . .

EVE'S VOICE

. . . and it was Karen who first brought me to one whom I had always idolized — and who was to become my benefactor and champion. A great actress and a great woman — Margo Channing.

MARGO

Part of Eve's tribute has been over her CLOSEUP. She smiles grimly in reaction to the applause.

EVE

She looks to her right, waits for the applause to die.

EVE

My director — who demanded always a little more than my talent could provide —

BILL

Seated at the speakers' table. He has his award before him — a smaller one. He puts out a cigarette expressionlessly as the applause breaks out.

EVE'S VOICE

— but who taught me patiently and well . . . Bill Sampson.

LLOYD

He sits beside Bill. He, too, has a smaller award. As Eve speaks, he throws her a brief glance.

EVE'S VOICE

And one, without whose great play and faith in me, this night would never have been. How can I repay Lloyd Richards?

EVE

Waits for the applause to die.

EVE

How can I repay the many others? So many, that I couldn't possibly name them all . . .

ADDISON

He smiles approvingly.

EVE'S VOICE

. . . whose help, guidance and advice have made this, the happiest night of my life, possible.

EVE

She stares at the award for an instant, as if fighting for self-control.

EVE

Although I am going to Hollywood next week to make a film — do not think for a moment that I am leaving you. How could I? For my heart is here in the Theatre — and three thousand miles are too far to be away from one's heart. I'll be back to claim it — and soon. That is, if you want me back.

Another storm of applause. Much ad-lib shouting as Bill and Lloyd are summoned to pose beside her for more pictures. People are thronging out. The aged actor shouts above the hubbub.

AGED ACTOR

A good night to all — and to all a good night!

Eve disengages herself from the photographers, makes her way toward Addison's table . . . Bill and Lloyd follow. CAMERA FOLLOWS Lloyd to Karen. They kiss. He gives her the award.

LLOYD

For services rendered — beyond the whatever-it-is of duty, darling . . .

Max bustles into their SHOT.

MAX

Come on! I'm the host, I gotta get home before the guests start stealing the liquor . . .

She and Lloyd follow Max. Addison and Eve are on their way. Lloyd goes right by. Karen pauses by Eve.

KAREN

Congratulations, Eve.

EVE

Thank you, Karen.

Karen goes. Eve is being constantly congratulated. Some ad libs about seeing her at Max's party. Margo and Bill step into the SHOT. Eve turns from a well-wisher to face her.

MARGO

. . . nice speech, Eve. But I wouldn't worry too much about your heart. You can always put that award where your heart ought to be.

Eve looks at her wordlessly. Margo and Bill leave. Addison and Eve are alone. The tables about them are empty.

Suddenly, her face becomes expressionless, her eyes dull . . . she glances at the table.

EVE

I don't suppose there's a drink left . . .

ADDISON

You can have one at Max's.

EVE

(sits)

I don't think I'm going.

ADDISON

(sighs)

Why not?

EVE

Because I don't want to.

ADDISON

(patiently)

Max has gone to a great deal of trouble, it's going to be an elaborate party, and it's for you.

EVE

No, it's not.

(she holds up the award)

It's for this.

ADDISON

It's the same thing, isn't it?

EVE

Exactly.

(she gives him the award)

Here. Take it to the party instead of me.

ADDISON

You're being childish.

A well-wisher rushes up to Eve with an "Eve, darling, I'm so happy for you!" Eve rises, thanks her graciously. Then she pulls her wrap over her shoulder.

EVE

I'm tired. I want to go home.

ADDISON

(curtly)

Very well. I shall drop you and go on to the party alone. I have no intention of missing it . . .

They exit from the room, now empty of everything but tables, waiters and the usual banquet debris.

DISSOLVE TO:

PARK AVE — NIGHT

Eve gets out of a taxi in front of a fashionable apartment

hotel. She doesn't say good night to Addison, she enters the hotel as the cab drives off. She *hasn't the award* with her.

DISSOLVE TO:

CORRIDOR OUTSIDE EVE'S APARTMENT — NIGHT

Smart, but not gaudy. Eve crosses from the elevator to her apartment. She lets herself in.

EVE'S HOTEL APARTMENT — NIGHT

A small foyer, from which one door leads to the living room, another to the bedroom. The bedroom and living room do not connect except through the foyer.

All the lights are out. Eve turns them on in the foyer, the same as she enters the bedroom. There are some new trunks, in various stages of being packed. Eve tosses her wrap on the bed, goes through the foyer to the living room.

She turns on the lights in the living room. CAMERA FOLLOWS her to a smart small bar where she fixes a stiff drink.

As she turns from the bar, she stares — starts in fright — and drops the drink.

A young girl, asleep in a chair, wakes with a jump. She stares at Eve, horror-stricken.

EVE

Who are you?

GIRL

Miss Harrington . . .

EVE

What are you doing here?

GIRL

I — I guess I fell asleep.

Eve starts for the phone. The girl rises in panic.

GIRL

Please don't have me arrested, please! I didn't steal anything — you can search me!

EVE

(pauses)

How did you get in here?

EVE

I hid outside in the hall till the maid came to turn down your bed. She must've forgot something and when she went to get it, she left the door open. I sneaked in and hid till she finished. Then I just looked around — and pretty soon I was afraid somebody'd notice the lights were on so I turned them off — and then I guess, I fell asleep.

EVE

You were just looking around . . .

GIRL

That's all.

EVE

What for?

GIRL

You probably won't believe me.

EVE

Probably not.

GIRL

It was for my report.

EVE

What report? To whom?

GIRL

About how you live, what kind of clothes you wear — what kind of perfume and books — things like that. You know the Eve Harrington Clubs — that they've got in most of the girls' high schools?

EVE

I've heard of them.

GIRL

Ours was one of the first. Erasmus Hall. I'm the president.

EVE

Erasmus Hall. That's in Brooklyn, isn't it?

GIRL

Lots of actresses came from Brooklyn. Barbara Stanwyck, Susan Hayward — of course, they're just movie stars.

Eve makes no comment. She lies wearily on a couch.

GIRL

You're going to Hollywood — aren't you?
(Eve murmurs "uh-huh")
From the trunks you're packing, you must be going to stay a long time.

EVE

I might.

GIRL

That spilled drink is going to ruin your carpet.

She crosses to it.

EVE

The maid'll fix it in the morning.

GIRL

I'll just pick up the broken glass . . .

EVE

Don't bother.

The girl puts the broken glass on the bar. She starts to mix Eve a fresh drink.

EVE

How'd you get all the way up here from Brooklyn?

GIRL

Subway.

EVE

How long does it take?

GIRL

With changing and everything, a little over an hour.

She carries the drink over to Eve.

EVE

It's after one now. You won't get home till all hours.

GIRL

(smiles)

I don't care if I never get home . . .

The door buzzer sounds.

EVE

That's the door.

GIRL

You rest. I'll get it.

She goes to the door, opens it. Addison stands there, the Sarah Siddons Award in his hands.

ADDISON

Hello, there. Who are you?

GIRL

(shyly)

Miss Harrington's resting, Mr. DeWitt. She asked me to see who it is.

ADDISON

We won't disturb her rest. It seems she left her award in the taxicab. Will you give it to her?

She holds it as if it were the Promised Land. Addison smiles faintly. He knows that look.

ADDISON

How do you know my name?

GIRL

It's a very famous name, Mr. DeWitt.

ADDISON

And what is your name?

GIRL

Phoebe.

ADDISON

Phoebe?

GIRL

(stubbornly)

I call myself Phoebe.

ADDISON

Why not? Tell me, Phoebe, do you want some day to have an award like that of your own?

Phoebe lifts her eyes to him.

PHOEBE

More than anything else in the world.

Addison pats her shoulder lightly.

ADDISON

Then you must ask Miss Harrington how to get one. Miss Harrington knows all about it . . .

Phoebe smiles shyly. Addison closes the door. Phoebe stares down at the award for an instant.

EVE'S VOICE

(sleepy — from the living room)

Who was it?

PHOEBE

Just a taxi driver, Miss Harrington. You left the award in his cab and he brought it back.

EVE'S VOICE

Oh. Put it on one of the trunks, will you? I want to pack it . . .

PHOEBE

Sure, Miss Harrington.

She takes the award into the bedroom, sets it on a trunk. As she starts out, she sees Eve's fabulous wrap on the bed. She listens. Then, quietly, she puts on the wrap and picks up the award.

Slowly, she walks to a large three-mirrored cheval. With grace and infinite dignity she holds the award to her, and bows again and again . . . as if to the applause of a multitude.

FADE OUT